The Illustrated NFL Playbook

An Official NFL Publication   Workman Publishing, New York

Written and produced by National Football League Properties, Creative Services Division.

Designed by David Johnston
Design Assistants: Laurel Burden, Felice Mataré
Cover and inside illustrations by Paul Kratter

Another National Football League book you will enjoy from Workman Publishing:
  National Football League Media Information Book

Workman Publishing Co.
1 West 39th Street, New York, N.Y. 10018
Manufactured in the United States of America.
First Printing, July, 1982

10 9 8 7 6 5 4 3 2 1

Contents

Introduction

It's easy to watch a pro football game and enjoy it; millions of people do each week during the NFL season. But the game is even better when the viewer—either at the stadium or watching on television—can get beneath the surface action and appreciate all the nuances, the subtleties, *the moves.*

A good path to appreciating anything is to try your hand at it. Running a 10-kilometer race can make a jogger marvel at the endurance of marathoners. Or, playing in a local tennis tournament can cause a weekend hacker to watch Wimbledon with new insight.

Unfortunately, some things are difficult, if not impossible, to try yourself. Few people, for example, will ever know how it feels to drive a Formula car at 150 miles per hour. And only a handful of people will ever cannonball down an Olympic downhill ski course.

Playing pro football also is an experience that relatively few can ever have. Yet, thanks to its tremendous popularity and exposure (or, perhaps, the reason for it), the NFL game is one of the most accessible of sports.

Reduced to abstract terms, pro football is action and reaction, ebb and flow, point and counterpoint. Momentum is gained and lost. Voids are created, then filled.

It is, as Vince Lombardi said, a game of basics—running and jumping, blocking and tackling, throwing and catching a uniquely-shaped ball.

These things came first. *Then* came the embellishments; the strategies, tactics, and techniques, compounding like interest over the years; zone defenses; gadget plays; blitzes, stunts, and dogs; option passes and bombs; spreads and Shotguns; flankers, I-backs, and designated pass rushers.

Pro football also is a game of personalities, a fact that sometimes gets lost in the double-header shuffle of uniforms across America's television screens on autumn Sundays. All the play diagrams and technical philosophies become moot without someone to make them come alive out on the field.

"We often make the error of thinking we can accomplish something simply by drawing Xs and Os," says Sid Gillman, a pro football mastermind and former NFL head coach (who helped immensely with the production of this book). "But those Xs and Os don't mean a thing if you don't have the people to carry them out."

Jack Faulkner of the Los Angeles Rams (another former NFL head coach and valued contributor) adds, "There's an old saying that you've got to be able to compete off the field before you can compete on the field. That means getting the right players."

By the "right players" Faulkner does not only mean the biggest, fastest, or strongest. He wants the brightest as well.

Football can be basically a simple game. But the way it is played in the NFL is anything but simple. A pro football team's playbook can be as thick as a major-city telephone directory. Leafing through such a playbook is probably the quickest way to gain respect for the mental requirements of the game.

Of course, fans also have to deal with similar information (though not nearly in such volume) in order to understand what's happening in a game. Hence *The Illustrated NFL Playbook.* It contains much of the same information as a team playbook only in a generic, condensed, and more readable form.

From watching NFL games in person or on television, most fans already have a good working knowledge of football terminology, basics, and rules. *The Illustrated NFL Playbook* was written to help fans at all levels of comprehension see *inside* the game as it is being played today, and to spotlight the newest wrinkles and trends that keep pro football in a constant state of refinement and evolution.

So, this is above all a fan's book. Think of it as a tourist's guide and a reference rather than a coaching text (which it certainly isn't). Clarity has been the watchword of its writing, production, and design; entertainment and education its goals.

Keep it beside your television set after you've read it. You never know when you're going to have to beat a strongside rotating zone.

Key to Illustrations

In order to make clear the action of plays used as examples, the following symbols and colors are used throughout this book:

- The defense always is blue.
- The offense always is gold.
- The key offensive and/or defensive players always are red.

Red arrows are for the movements of key players.

A solid red figure indicates position at the snap of the ball.

A red outline indicates position prior to going in motion.

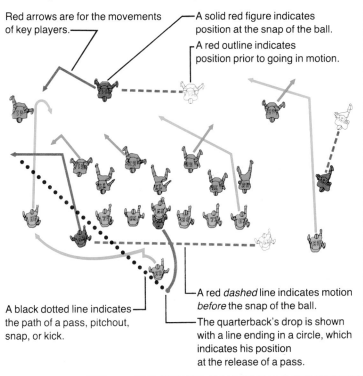

A black dotted line indicates the path of a pass, pitchout, snap, or kick.

A red *dashed* line indicates motion *before* the snap of the ball.

The quarterback's drop is shown with a line ending in a circle, which indicates his position at the release of a pass.

The defense always is blue. The offense always is gold. Key players always are red.

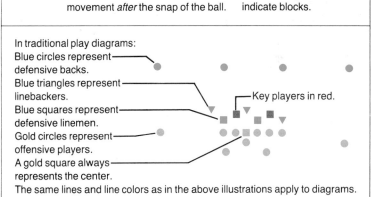

Arrows are used to indicate movement *after* the snap of the ball.

Lines ending in a T-bar indicate blocks.

In traditional play diagrams:
Blue circles represent defensive backs.
Blue triangles represent linebackers.
Blue squares represent defensive linemen.
Gold circles represent offensive players.
A gold square always represents the center.

Key players in red.

The same lines and line colors as in the above illustrations apply to diagrams.

The Basics

Once during a Green Bay Packers offensive slump, head coach Vince Lombardi called a team meeting. "We're going back to basics," he said. *"Back to fundamentals.*

"Now this," he said, holding up a ball, "is a football."

"Hold on, coach," interrupted split end Max McGee. "You're going too fast."

The Ball

Lombardi was right; the football is the game's most *basic* basic. It gives the game its name, and its unusual shape makes the action of the sport unique. The whole object of the game, after all, is to pass it, run with it, and cross the other team's goal line with it in your possession (or kick it through the goal posts) in order to score more points than your opponent.

The football used in NFL play is manufactured by the Wilson Sporting Goods Company of Ada, Ohio. It retails for approximately $40, and bears the signature of NFL Commissioner Pete Rozelle. It is an inflated rubber bladder (in the shape of a prolate spheroid) filled with 12½ to 13½ pounds of air, enclosed in a pebble-grained leather (not pigskin, as is commonly believed) case of natural tan color, and weighs 14 to 15 ounces.

There are 24 footballs available at every NFL game, provided by the home team.

The Field

The types of playing surfaces vary from stadium to stadium in the NFL (and are almost evenly divided between natural grass and artificial turf), but one thing remains consistent throughout the league—the size, shape, and markings of the field.

An NFL field is a rectangle measuring 120 yards long by 53⅓ yards wide. (The unusual width was established by football pioneer Walter Camp of Yale in the late 1800s. Under pressure to reduce injuries by opening up the game with a larger field, Camp had to settle for 53⅓ because that was the largest width that would fit in the new stadium at Harvard.) The actual field of play is 100 by 53⅓ yards. The field is bounded on both sides by the **side-**

> **Chuck Noll on Football:**
> *"The nice thing about football is that you have a scoreboard to show you how you've done. In other things in life, you don't. At least not one you can see."*

lines and at both ends by two 10-yard areas known as the **end zones,** which also are bounded by the sidelines, **goal lines,** and **end lines.** In each end zone there are goal posts, set 10 yards behind the goal line on the end line, which are used to determine accuracy on field goal and extra point attempts.

Between the goal lines, the field is sectioned off with white lines (known as yard lines) at intervals of five yards, culminating at the center of the field, the 50 yard line, also called the midfield stripe. This gives each team 50 yards of territory and a goal line to defend.

There are two easy ways to tell which team's side of the field the ball is on. One is to remember that the team on **offense** (the team with the ball) always tries to advance *away* from its own goal line (and toward the goal line of the team on **defense**). The other method is to look at the directional arrows painted on the field beside each field number (except the 50); they point toward the nearest goal line.

The short (4 inches wide by 2 feet long) lines, inset 70 feet 9 inches from the sidelines on either side of the field and running its length in one-yard intervals, are called **hashmarks.** They are used by the officials to **spot** (place) the ball before each play.

Another important line is the **line of scrimmage.** This is whatever line on which the ball rests as it faces the defensive team. The offensive team and defensive team assemble on either side of this line to begin a

The Field

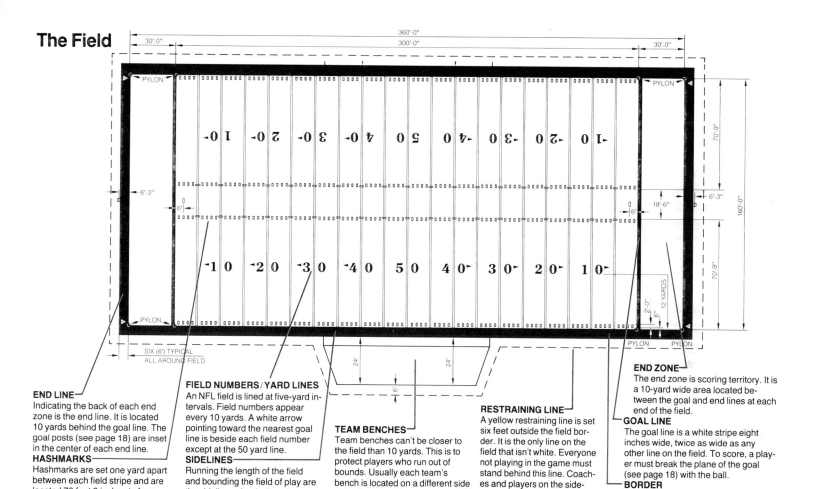

END LINE
Indicating the back of each end zone is the end line. It is located 10 yards behind the goal line. The goal posts (see page 18) are inset in the center of each end line.

HASHMARKS
Hashmarks are set one yard apart between each field stripe and are located 70 feet 9 inches in from each sideline. They are used by officials for spotting the ball.

FIELD NUMBERS/YARD LINES
An NFL field is lined at five-yard intervals. Field numbers appear every 10 yards. A white arrow pointing toward the nearest goal line is beside each field number except at the 50 yard line.

SIDELINES
Running the length of the field and bounding the field of play are the sidelines. Any ball or player going beyond the sideline is considered out of bounds.

TEAM BENCHES
Team benches can't be closer to the field than 10 yards. This is to protect players who run out of bounds. Usually each team's bench is located on a different side of the field. But, if the home team wants, both teams' benches can be located on the same side.

RESTRAINING LINE
A yellow restraining line is set six feet outside the field border. It is the only line on the field that isn't white. Everyone not playing in the game must stand behind this line. Coaches and players on the sidelines must stay in an area between the two 32 yard lines during a game.

END ZONE
The end zone is scoring territory. It is a 10-yard wide area located between the goal and end lines at each end of the field.

GOAL LINE
The goal line is a white stripe eight inches wide, twice as wide as any other line on the field. To score, a player must break the plane of the goal (see page 18) with the ball.

BORDER
A six-foot wide white border goes around the field and end lines. It aids in out-of-bounds calls and in player safety.

9

The Teams

● **OFFENSE**

● **DEFENSE**

FULLBACK
An extremely powerful runner who lines up to the tight end's side and usually gets the "bread and butter" assignments. Also expected to be a good blocker and pass receiver. Fullbacks and halfbacks are not distinguished in some offenses; they are simply designated **running backs**.

HALFBACK
The "handyman" of the team. He runs, blocks, receives, and sometimes throws passes.

WIDE RECEIVER
Usually the team's fastest receivers (pass catchers). They are "split"—stationed several yards from the interior linemen.

TIGHT END
The tight end (stationed next to the tackle) must be bigger and stronger than most receivers. Because of the extra blocking power he adds to the line, the side of the offensive formation the tight end lines up on is called the **strongside**. The side without the tight end is called the **weakside**. Defenses set up accordingly.

WIDE RECEIVER
(see below)

TACKLE
(see below)

GUARD
(see below)

QUARTERBACK
The man in charge. He calls signals, is the primary passer and ball handler, and occasionally runs the ball.

END
(see above)

CENTER, GUARDS, AND TACKLES
It is *these* five men—one center, two guards (right and left) who line up on either side of the center, and two tackles (right and left) who line up outside the guards—who make up the **interior line**.

TACKLES AND ENDS
Called the **front four** in a 4-3 set (shown here). They are the largest men on defense because their jobs are (1) stop the running attack and (2) rush the passer. Defensive linemen line up on the line of scrimmage and are permitted to use their hands against blockers.

In a 3-4 alignment, there are two ends and a middle man, called a **nose tackle**; the fourth lineman is replaced by an additional linebacker.

LINEBACKERS
The defensive team's version of the "handymen." They must pursue running plays, drop back and defend against passes, or disrupt pass plays with all-out rushes from their positions called **dogs** and **blitzes**.

CORNERBACKS AND SAFETIES
Also called **defensive backs**, they operate in the area of the defense called the **secondary**. They are required to tackle much bigger runners, yet on pass plays, they must have the speed to catch the fastest receivers. They also blitz.

CORNERBACK
(see above)

play from scrimmage. The space measuring the length of the ball, between the two teams, is called the **neutral zone;** neither team may enter it until the play begins.

Game Time

A game is divided into four quarters, each 15 minutes long. The first two quarters are called the first half, the third and fourth the second half. (If a game is tied when time runs out, an extra 15-minute **overtime** period is played; in postseason games, as many periods as necessary are played until one team scores to win.)

Between halves there is a 15-minute intermission called halftime during which the teams leave the field to rest and discuss strategy.

Both halves of the game begin with a kickoff. At the *end* of the first and third quarters, there are intervals of two minutes. There is no subsequent kickoff and the players do not leave after these intervals. Instead, they exchange directions on the field. This prevents either team from realizing any advantage from prevailing weather conditions; the sun's glare or the wind's direction could be major factors in determining the outcome of the game.

In addition to the preceding pauses in the action, each team is permitted to call three 90-second **time outs** during *each* half. Time outs (so called because the game clock is stopped) generally are called on the field by a team's offensive and defensive captains, or other designated players. Time outs also are

called by the officials to assess penalties, measure for yardage gained, replace equipment, tend to any injured players, and to inform the benches that two minutes remain in the second and fourth quarters of the game (called the **two-minute warning**).

As well as having to deal with the running time of the official game clock, the offensive team faces one more time constraint: the **30-second clock.** Each offensive play must begin within 30 seconds of the referee's whistle (signaling that the ball is ready for play) or the offensive team is penalized. A mistake such as letting the 30-second clock expire is costly, and at the end of a close game it can be critical.

Player Numbers

All NFL players are numbered according to their positions*:

1-19	Quarterbacks and kickers
20-49	Running backs and defensive backs
50-59	Centers and linebackers
60-79	Defensive linemen and interior offensive linemen
80-89	Wide receivers and tight ends
90-99	Defensive linemen

All players who had been in the National Football League prior to 1972 may use their old numbers.

The Teams

There are 45 players currently allowed on an NFL roster. From these players, each team organizes different 11-man units—the of-

fense, the **defense,** and **special teams** (used on kickoffs, punts, field goals, and extra points).

The starting offensive unit (see chart, opposite) breaks down into the **line** (blockers), consisting of a center, two guards, and two tackles;

NFL Rosters by Position

Here's how an average 45-man NFL roster breaks down in terms of number of players per position:

Offensive linemen	8
Receivers	6
Running backs	5
Quarterbacks	3
Defensive linemen	6
Linebackers	8
Defensive backs	7
Kicker	1
Punter	1
	45

GAME TRENDS

THREE QUARTERBACKS ON THE ROSTER.

Since the advent of the 16-game schedule in 1978, more and more teams have been keeping three, instead of two, quarterbacks on their rosters. Though new rules have been instituted to protect quarterbacks, the longer schedule increases the possibility of injury. Most teams try for an ideal balance among their three quarterbacks, retaining an active starter, an experienced back-up, and a young future starting prospect.

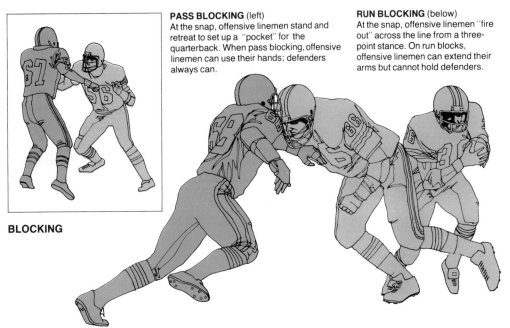

PASS BLOCKING (left)
At the snap, offensive linemen stand and retreat to set up a "pocket" for the quarterback. When pass blocking, offensive linemen can use their hands; defenders always can.

RUN BLOCKING (below)
At the snap, offensive linemen "fire out" across the line from a three-point stance. On run blocks, offensive linemen can extend their arms but cannot hold defenders.

BLOCKING

the **receivers** (pass catchers), usually consisting of two wide receivers and a tight end (more than one tight end may be used depending on the formation); and the **backfield,** consisting of the quarterback and two running backs, who also are eligible receivers.

The starting defensive unit can be broken down into the **line,** consisting of three or four linemen (depending on the situation); the **linebackers** (three or four, again depending on the situation); and the **secondary,** consisting of two cornerbacks and two safeties, who are primarily pass defenders.

Every team also has a head coach and a staff of assistant coaches (the number varies with the team), who each specialize in working with certain positions (e.g. receivers, offensive line, linebackers) or areas of strategy (offensive and defensive coordinators).

Measuring Progress

Not more than three minutes before the opening kickoff, a coin toss is held to determine who will have first possession of the ball. The referee (the official in the black hat) meets with the captains of both teams for the coin toss. While the coin is in the air, the captain of the visiting team makes the call (heads or tails). The winner of the toss chooses either to kick off or receive, or which goal his team will defend. For the second half, the captain who lost the pregame toss has the first choice.

Progress in a football game is measured in yards. Any time a team is on offense, it is given four chances, or **downs,** to gain 10 yards. If it advances the ball this distance or more, it makes a **first down.** This means it retains the ball and the right to four more downs. A team that fails to make a first down in three tries usually **punts** (kicks) the ball downfield on fourth down and the other side gets its chance to go on offense. If on fourth down, a team tries to make a first down and fails, the other team gets the ball where the play was stopped.

The offensive team's situation—the down and the distance it has to go to make a first down— can be expressed verbally. The situation of a team on second down with seven yards to go for a first down, for example, is said to be "second and seven."

Downs are measured carefully by two men officially known as linesmen (unofficially, "the chain gang"), who are stationed along the sidelines. They carry two rods to which is

Basic NFL Offensive Formations

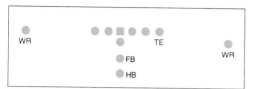

I-FORMATION: Both running backs line up in a straight line behind the quarterback. This is a good running formation, particularly for a running back who can pick his own holes.

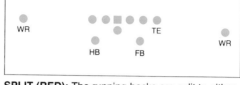

SPLIT (RED): The running backs are split to either side of the quarterback; the better blocker of the two lines up to the strongside for extra power.

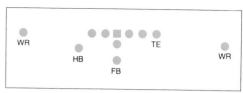

DOUBLE WING: The better receiver of the two running backs lines up a yard outside the tackle and two yards behind the line of scrimmage to get free more quickly on a pass pattern. The other back lines up behind the quarterback.

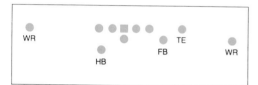

TRIPLE WING: One running back lines up between the tight end and the tackle; the other back splits to the weakside. This puts three receivers to the strongside.

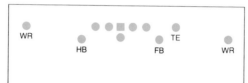

SPREAD: The combination of one back in the double-wing position and the other in the triple-wing position. Five receivers are available quickly.

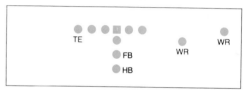

SLOT: Both wide receivers line up on one side; the tight end goes to the other. The running backs can line up in any formation (the I is shown).

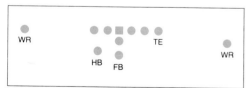

OPPOSITE (BROWN): The fullback (power runner) is behind the quarterback; the halfback splits slightly to the weakside. This formation is often used to run to the weakside.

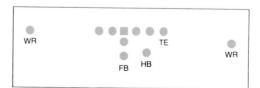

NEAR (BLUE): The fullback is behind the quarterback and the halfback splits slightly to the strongside. Some teams use a second tight end with this formation to get blocking power both ways, particularly in goal line or short-yardage situations.

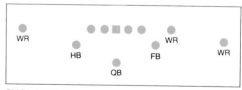

SHOTGUN: Similar to the spread, except that the quarterback takes the snap standing between five and seven yards deep in the backfield. This is primarily a passing formation.

attached a chain that is exactly 10 yards long. The chain is stretched its full length from the line of scrimmage. If *any portion* of the ball is advanced beyond the chain, it's a first down.

The linesmen are accompanied by another man who carries a pole with large flip-cards on top. These cards are numbered 1-2-3-4 and simply indicate which down is being played.

At the Line

Each down consists of a play, a set plan of action carried out by the offense on which each player has certain responsibilities. Plays are called—though not necessarily *selected*—by the quarterback in a **huddle** with the team grouped around him about seven yards behind the ball. Exactly which play will be used on the upcoming down is generally decided by coaches on the sideline and in the press box. Plays are sent in to the quarterback either by hand signals from the sideline or with a player coming into the game.

There are four good reasons for the coach to select the play: 1. He has years of experience in football; 2. He calls the plays in practice; 3. He supervises the analysis of the opponent's game films; and, 4. Knowing the play, he can alert his assistants in the press box to it before it is run, so they can watch how it is defensed.

In the huddle, the quarterback calls the play, which consists of: 1. The **formation** (placement of players) to be used; 2. Whether the tight end is to line up on the left or right; 3. The exact action of the play; and 4. The **snap count** (the number on which the ball will be handed, or snapped, by the center to the quarterback to begin the play). Then he says, "Break!"

Here is an example:

<blockquote>
Formation: Red Right
Play: 28
Snap Count: on 3
Break!
</blockquote>

When the huddle breaks, each player goes to his assigned spot in the formation. The quarterback gets set behind the center and calls signals (number and word codes), which include: 1. The defense that the opponent is playing; 2. A color and a number; 3. The color and number once again; 4. "Down!"; and, 5. A series of non-rhythmic hikes.

Here is an example:

<blockquote>
Defense: Thirty-four
Color and Number: Orange 19, Orange 19.
Down!
Hike!…Hike! Hike!
</blockquote>

The color and number are so important that they are repeated. Each week, a different color is "live." If the quarterback looks over (**reads**) the defense and feels that the play called in the huddle will not work, he has the option of calling an **audible,** which changes the play at the line of scrimmage. He alerts his players to the change by shouting the "live" color (some teams use a repeat of the snap count number instead of a color), and then follows it with the number of the new play. But most of the time, the color the quarterback calls is a "dummy call."

The quarterback uses the word "hike" instead of saying "One, two, three." That is, a play with a snap count of two will start on the second "hike." The hikes are called out in a non-rhythmic cadence to keep the defense off-balance.

Sometimes, in order to get a play off quickly before the defense has a chance to adjust, the play will be called on a **quick count.** When this happens, the usual signals are abbreviated. A variation of the quick count is **going on sound;** the center snaps the ball on the first sound the quarterback utters.

An experienced quarterback, by altering his cadence, often can make the defensive team jump into the neutral zone and cause it to be penalized. If the quarterback does this too obviously, he may himself be penalized.

Moving the Ball

Once a team takes possession of the football, there are several ways it can make or gain yardage (advance the ball toward the other team's goal line).

RUNNING. Technically, any offensive player can run with the ball, but it is the running backs who almost always do it. Wide receivers and tight ends also occasionally are ball carriers.

Getting the Ball to the Backs

HANDOFF   FLARE PASS   PITCHOUT

So are the quarterbacks, though they generally run on very short yardage situations or when forced to by the defensive pass rush.

Running plays begin with the snap from center. The quarterback then turns and gives the ball to one of the running backs (a **handoff**). On some plays, the quarterback fakes a handoff to one running back, then gives the ball to the other. A variation of the handoff is the **pitchout,** an underhand toss most often used as a means of getting the ball to the carrier on a running play that is sweeping wide.

Runs can go **outside** (the area between the offensive tackle and the sideline), **inside** (the

area between the two offensive tackles), or **up the middle** (over center).

While on the subject of running, occasionally you will see one of the backs begin to run in the direction of the sideline *before* the ball is snapped. This **man in motion** is perfectly legal. Only one man on offense is permitted to be in motion before the ball is snapped, and he is required to run in a lateral—*not forward*—direction. Everyone else on the offense must be completely still for one full second before the snap. Defensive players, however, are free to shift and move as they please.

PASSING. Any offensive player can throw

a pass, but it is the quarterback who does it almost exclusively. On a passing play, the quarterback takes the snap, drops back (retreats) five to seven yards into the **pocket** (the circle of protection provided by his blockers), and scans the field to see if his receivers are open (free of defenders) or covered by defenders. Also at the snap, defensive linemen (and/or sometimes linebackers and secondary men), seeing a pass play developing, charge across the line of scrimmage (make **penetration**) in an effort to get to the quarterback before he can throw. If a quarterback is forced from the pocket by this

Eligible Pass Receivers

Only certain offensive players are eligible to catch passes (indicated in red). Any defensive player, however, may intercept and return a pass.

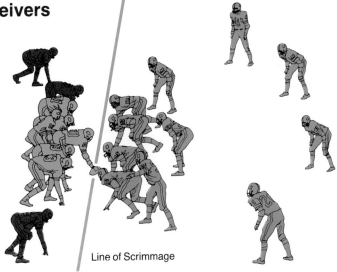

Line of Scrimmage

defensive **pass rush** before he can get the pass off, he has to run (**scramble**) to get away from the pressure. If the quarterback is tackled behind the line, it is called a **quarterback sack.**

For purposes of deception, most teams have another man in the backfield who throws the ball well. Thus, on a "halfback option play," the halfback begins running with the ball. He may choose to continue his running or he may pass the ball. But once the ball has crossed the line of scrimmage on a play, it may not be legally passed forward.

The eligible offensive receivers are those players who are on either end of the offensive line, and players who are at least one yard behind the line at the snap of the ball, except the quarterback. Or to put it another way, the only men who are not permitted to catch passes are the interior linemen—the tackles, guards, and center—and the quarterback (if he has handled the ball on a direct snap from center).

Passes may be caught anywhere within the boundaries of the field of play. In order for a pass to be ruled **complete,** receivers must have the ball clearly in their possession and have *both* feet clearly inbounds.

There are other eligible receivers on the field that the quarterback does his best *not* to throw to—the defense. Any time a pass is thrown, defenders have as equal a right to catch it as offensive receivers. An offensive receiver and a defender may not physically hinder each other's attempt to catch a pass. If either does, the officials can rule it **pass interference**. When a pass is caught by a defensive player instead of the intended offensive receiver, the pass has been **intercepted**. Hence the old football saying that when a pass is thrown, three things can happen and two of them (interceptions and incompletions) are bad. However, in view of today's heavily pass-oriented offenses, modern coaches don't give much credence to that axiom.

The **forward pass** is just what its name implies; the ball is thrown forward. If it is not caught, it is an incomplete pass and the game clock is stopped. Play resumes at the line of scrimmage but the down is increased by one. Only one forward pass is permitted per down.

There are long passes (more than 20 yards deep, or downfield), short passes (less than 10 yards deep), sideline passes, and passes over the middle (usually 10-20 yards deep). There also are passes thrown in the backfield from the quarterback to the running backs called **flare passes,** or safety valve passes. When a running back catches a flare pass, he is usually out in the **flat,** the backfield area close to the sidelines.

A **lateral** pass usually occurs in the backfield when the ball carrier sees that he is about to be stopped by the defense. If he spots a teammate behind him, the ball carrier may lateral the ball to him in an effort to keep the play going. If a lateral is *not* caught, it is considered a free ball and can be advanced by the defense if it catches the ball before it touches the ground. If the defense recovers a lateral after the ball touches the ground, it retains possession at the spot of the recovery. **Fumbles** (a loss of possession of the ball by the ball carrier or handler) and interceptions can be advanced by the defense at any time. Similar to a fumble is a **muff,** which is the touching of the ball by a player in an *unsuccessful* attempt to obtain possession of a free ball. It is illegal to try to advance the ball by muffing or batting it forward.

KICKING. A **punt** is a type of kick (see illustration) normally used on a fourth-down play when a team has long yardage to make and/or is on its own side of the 50 yard line. The punter is called in to kick the ball deep into enemy territory *away from* his team's goal line.

The punter stands about 15 yards behind the line of scrimmage. He catches the ball as it is snapped back by the center, steps forward as he drops the ball, and kicks it *before* it touches the ground.

The other most common kicks used in football are of the **placekick** variety (see illustration). That is, the ball is kicked as it rests *in place* on the ground rather than being kicked

Types of Kicks

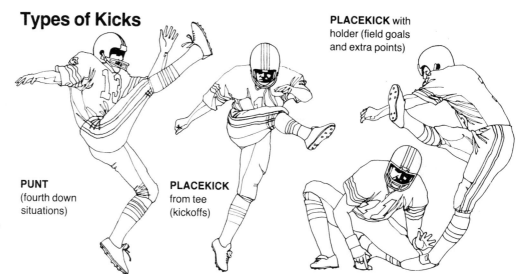

PUNT
(fourth down situations)

PLACEKICK
from tee
(kickoffs)

PLACEKICK with holder (field goals and extra points)

in mid-air in the style of a punt.

This method (having the ball remain stationary, usually resting on a tee) is used on kickoffs, the maneuver employed to put the ball in play at the beginning of the first and second halves of the game. Also, following any scoring play (except a safety), the team that scored must kick off to its opponent. After a safety (see scoring section) the team *scored upon* must kick to the scoring team. In this case, the **free kick** can be either a punt or a placekick. (Other types of placekicks—field goals and extra points—require a player to take the snap and hold the ball for the kicker. They will be discussed in the scoring section.)

PENALTIES. The ball also is advanced or set back by means of penalty assessments. A penalty usually ranges from 5-15 yards and/or loss of down, depending on the infraction and the situation when it takes place. When a penalty is called, one of the seven officials on the field throws his yellow marker, called a **flag.** The referee then discusses the options with the non-penalized team's captain and signals to the crowd what penalty was called, on whom it was called, and what the penalty assessment will be (see page 112).

STOPPING PLAY. Once a play of any kind has begun, there are six common ways it can end: a team scores; the ball carrier is tackled; the ball carrier goes out of bounds; a pass is ruled incomplete; the ball changes possession (through either a punt, fumble, or interception), or a penalty is called.

Scoring

In the NFL, teams can score in the following four ways: Six points for a **touchdown**

(1) when a runner with the ball crosses or touches his opponent's goal line, or (2) when a player catches a pass or recovers a loose ball within the boundaries of his opponent's end zone.

After a touchdown, the scoring team gets to try for an **extra point** (point after touchdown). The ball is placed two yards from the oppo-

nent's goal line. To earn that single point on which many games have turned, the team may (1) placekick or drop kick the ball through the *top* half of the goal post (above the cross-bar and between the uprights) or, infrequently, (2) run or pass the ball across the goal line in the same manner as a touchdown.

A third method of scoring—the three-point **field goal**—also involves the kicker and can be attempted from anywhere on the field (but is rarely tried from more than 50 yards away). However, field goals are much more difficult to make than extra points simply because the distance is much greater (don't forget the distance from the goal line to the goal post adds 10 yards to a field goal.)

The final, and least common, method of scoring is the **safety,** which has no relation to the player position of the same name. Two points for a safety are awarded to the team whose defensive unit tackles an offensive ball carrier *behind* his own goal line. A safety can also be scored when an offensive player is called for an infraction behind the goal line (such as holding) or if the ball is snapped, carried, or fumbled behind the end line. A play in which a snapped ball hits a goal post is also ruled a safety.

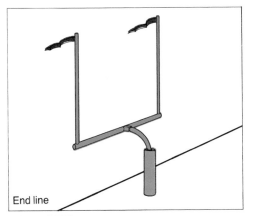

End line

GOAL POSTS

All goal posts, which are inset from the end line, used in the NFL are the same size and type, and are bright yellow in color. They also must be padded (to protect players) and have a ribbon 4 inches wide by 42 inches long attached to the top of each upright. The ribbons are there to show kickers which way the wind is blowing. Behind each goal post is a large net to catch kicks. The nets protect the crowd from being hit by kicked balls and keep game balls from being lost.

Goal line

THE PLANE OF THE GOAL

The goal line is not just a line on the field, it represents a *plane* (an imaginary wall extending straight up from the goal line). To score, a player only has to break the plane of the goal line with the ball. So, for example, a player who dives toward the end zone and crosses the plane of the goal line in the air has scored—even if he is pushed back and lands on the 1 yard line. A player also can score by reaching with the ball to break the goal plane, as long as the ball is in his possession and he is not yet down.

Scoring			
Touchdown	**6** points	Extra Point	**1** point
Field Goal	**3** points	Safety	**2** points

Basic NFL Defensive Formations

The two most common NFL defenses take their names from the numbers of linemen and linebackers present in each alignment.

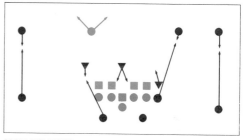

THE 4-3
The 4-3 defense features four defensive linemen (two ends and two tackles) and three linebackers (a middle linebacker and two outside linebackers).

THE 3-4
The 3-4 defense features three defensive linemen (a nose tackle in the middle, flanked by two defensive ends) and four linebackers (two outside and two inside).

Basic Pass Defenses

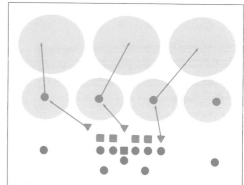

MAN-TO-MAN
In man-to-man coverage (pass defense), each defensive back is responsible for covering a specific offensive receiver; the defender follows him through his pass route.

ZONE
In a zone defense, pass defenders, including linebackers, are responsible for covering specific areas of the field (zones); they cover any receiver(s) entering that territory.

Where Officials Stand

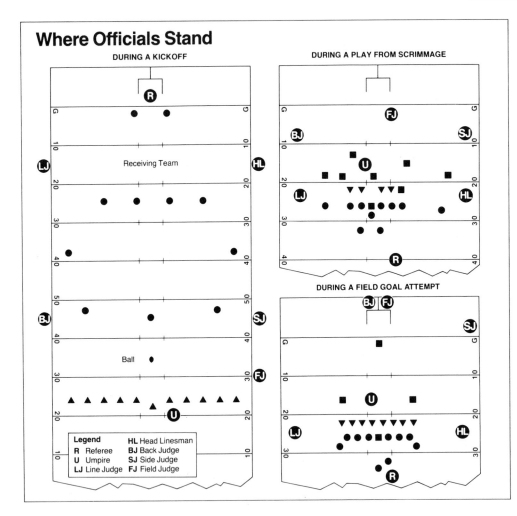

DURING A KICKOFF

Receiving Team

Ball

DURING A PLAY FROM SCRIMMAGE

DURING A FIELD GOAL ATTEMPT

Legend

R Referee	**HL** Head Linesman	
U Umpire	**BJ** Back Judge	
LJ Line Judge	**SJ** Side Judge	
	FJ Field Judge	

The Officials

Norm Schachter on Officials:
"While the official is an integral and vital part of the NFL, and of its individual games, the degree of anonymity he can achieve in front of 60,000 persons is a mark of his success."

In addition to the opposing offenses and defenses, there is a third team on the field at every NFL game—the officials. There are seven officials, each with his own area of responsibility. They are as follows:

REFEREE. He has general control of the game and final authority on rules interpretations. He determines the legality of the snap, observes backs for legal motion, drops back with the passer to determine the legality of line blocking, checks the legality of quarterbacks and rushers, and observes the punter and whether contact by a defender is legal.

UMPIRE. He rules primarily on players' equipment and their conduct on the scrimmage line. He observes the legality of blocking by the offensive line and watches for a possible false start by its members. He also watches defensive linemen as they ward off blocks and is responsible for detection of movement downfield by offensive linemen on pass plays.

HEAD LINESMAN. He rules on offside, encroachment, and action at the scrimmage line prior to and at the snap. He has full responsibility for ruling on sideline plays to his side, helps keep track of the down, and is in charge of the chain crew. He assists in determining a runner's forward progress and signals the forward point of the ball.

LINE JUDGE. He keeps time of the game as a backup for the clock operator. He rules whether passes are forward or backward, and whether the passer was behind the scrimmage line. He also watches for offside, encroachment, and actions at the scrimmage line prior to and at the snap. After a pass, he watches activity in the area behind the umpire. He keys the wide receiver to his side.

BACK JUDGE. He keys the tight end, or the near back if the tight end is on the opposite side. He watches the tight end or back for legality of blocks or actions taken against either. He calls clipping on punt returns, rules on legality of catches or pass interference, and rules on whether a runner or receiver is in or out of bounds. He lines up on the same side as the line judge, 15 to 17 yards deep.

FIELD JUDGE. He's 22 to 25 yards downfield, favoring the head linesman's side. He keys the tight end, or the near back if the tight end is on the opposite side. He watches for legality of their blocks or actions taken against them. He times the 30-second interval between plays and intermission between periods, and calls pass interference, fair catch infractions, and clipping on kick returns.

SIDE JUDGE. The side judge is the NFL's new-est official, added prior to the 1978 season. He stands on the same side as the head linesman, 17 yards deep. He assists the referee in decisions involving any catching, recovery, out of bounds spot, or illegal touching of a loose ball after it's crossed the scrimmage line, particularly when they occur out of viewing range of the line judge and umpire.

Most Common Official Signals

When something happens on the field that involves the officials, the referee communicates what has happened to the fans, and the television audience, via a microphone and a set of hand signals.

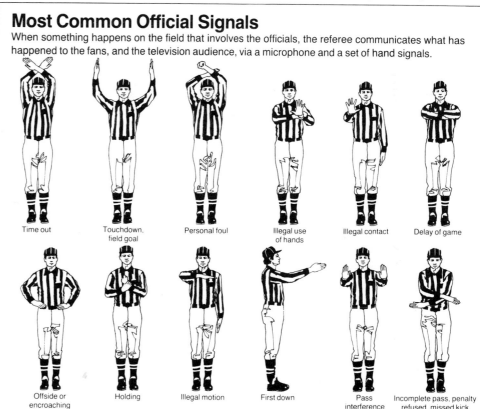

Time out

Touchdown, field goal

Personal foul

Illegal use of hands

Illegal contact

Delay of game

Offside or encroaching

Holding

Illegal motion

First down

Pass interference

Incomplete pass, penalty refused, missed kick

Offense

Rushing

Run Blocking

When running back O.J. Simpson of the Buffalo Bills broke the NFL record for yards gained in a season (2,003) in 1973, he made sure his offensive linemen were around him sharing the limelight during the postgame press conference.

Walter Payton of the Chicago Bears gave watches as "thank you" gifts to his linemen after the 1977 season, when he led the NFL in rushing.

And Tony Dorsett of the Dallas Cowboys gave pairs of cowboy boots, which he won in a Dallas player of the week program, to his offensive linemen.

These great running backs were not simply being generous or humble. Like all NFL rushers—superstars and journeymen alike—they recognize that without their blockers they would not get very far with the football.

Everyone blocks on the offensive unit. Of course, players at some positions—linemen, tight ends, and fullbacks in particular—are more formidable at the art than others. There are not comparative statistics, such as yards gained or tackles made, to single out exceptional blockers. But there *are* game films; coaches watch them to see blockers in action and grade players on their blocking perfor-

PULLING LINEMEN

Interior linemen in the NFL cannot rely on their size and strength alone to be successful blockers. They also must be able to run fast for short distances and, above all, they must be quick. These abilities merge in a maneuver critical to the offense's running game, called pulling. When a lineman pulls, he leaves his position at the snap and runs parallel to the line of scrimmage in the running lane either to lead a running back downfield or to trap block (see page 31) a defender. Guards do most of the pulling, but tackles and, occasionally, the center pull as well.

Running Lane

mances. A block does not have to be aesthetic, and a blocker does not have to exhibit textbook form to grade out well. He just has to get the job done—make room for the runner.

The Other Quarterback

The quarterback isn't the only offensive player who calls signals. The center makes line calls, which help the offensive line cope with shifts by the defense. Line calls essentially tell the offensive linemen who to block and how to block them; the man right across the line or the man at an angle to the right or left.

Even with all the shifting the defense is allowed to do before the snap of the ball, the offensive linemen still retain two distinct advantages—they know the snap count and they know where the play is going.

Whether a lineman gets a call or not, or, if a last-second defensive shift nullifies a line call, he has a contingency plan for every situation. This is rule blocking, blocking according to a predetermined set of guidelines.

For example, a play is called requiring the tight end and tackle to double-team the defensive end. Then the defense shifts into a formation with a linebacker moving in directly behind the defensive end. The rule for the tight end in this situation is to block the first linebacker to the inside. Because of the defensive alignment, the double-team block is off; the offensive tackle takes the defensive end by himself, and the tight end follows the rule and angles in on the linebacker.

Blocking Patterns

The most basic type of line blocking is the traditional power, drive, or straight-ahead blocking. In this scheme, offensive linemen block the man lined up directly across the line of scrimmage. This type of blocking can't always be used because defensive linemen don't always line up nose-to-nose over offensive linemen and because of the proliferation of defensive linemen with too much size, speed, and explosive strength for one man to handle alone.

Consequently, offenses employ blocking combinations; precisely timed variations of single- and double-team assaults, to improve angles and set up easier targets.

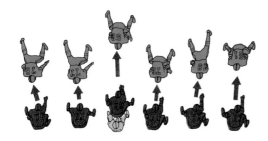

POWER: Straight-ahead blocking; linemen fire out at men directly over them.

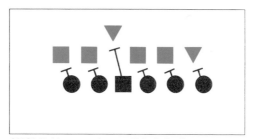

ANGLE: Linemen slant and block the first man to the right or left.

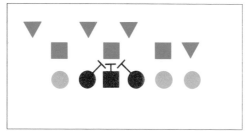

WEDGE: Three blockers converge on one defender; commonly used on the nose tackle in the 3-4.

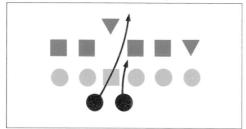

LEAD: One running back leads the other through the hole in the line.

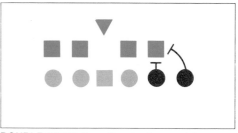

DOUBLE-TEAM: Two offensive linemen take on one defender.

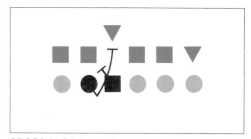

CROSS BLOCK: Two linemen exchange blocking assignments (also called scissors).

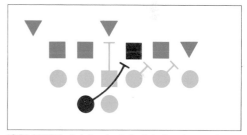

ISOLATION: A defender is isolated and a running back picks him off.

Running Inside

Inside running is the power game. It is the type of running at which ball control offenses excel, directed up the middle in the area of the line between the guards where first downs are made the hard way.

Teams also go inside for strategic reasons, such as using quick hitters (inside running plays run on short counts) to make defensive linemen and linebackers stay home (slow down their pass rushes or outside pursuit). Even the most pass-oriented offense must establish a running attack early in a game or the defense, realizing it does not have to contend with the threat of a ground attack, will be coming (rushing hard) every play.

A key to all phases of offenses, but particularly rushing offense, is the use of formations that force the set of the defense and put players in position for angle blocking. Many NFL teams line up in one offensive formation then shift into a completely different one.

HOLE NUMBERING AND PLAY CALLING

Each hole, or space, between or beside the interior linemen is designated by a number; odd numbers to the left, even to the right. The *spaces* the running backs stand in also are numbered —2 to the left, 3 directly behind the quarterback, and 4 to the right. The backs are designated by the number of the space they are set in, regardless of whether they're a halfback or a fullback. The quarterback always is the 1 back. This hole and back numbering system allows play calling to become verbal shorthand. For example, if the play is to have the halfback (the "2" back in the formation below) go through the hole off-tackle right (the "6" hole), the quarterback would call for a "26" play.

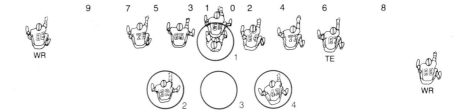

OPTION RUNNING

It used to be that running backs were expected to go through the assigned hole no matter what the obstacle. Now, teams like to have at least one back who can pick his own alternative holes should the blocking not materialize at the planned point of attack. A good option runner is a problem for defenses. Even if defenders react correctly to the play's action, an option runner may veer into another hole, or reverse his field and cut back against the flow—and pursuit—of the play.

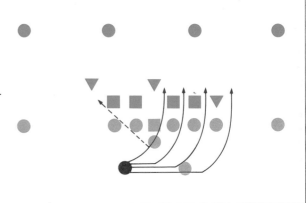

Running Outside

Two of the most basic running plays in football are the off-tackle slant and the sweep. Going off-tackle was considered the signature play in the NFL for many years and, to some coaches, it still is. Even if it isn't a modern coach's favorite play, off-tackle runs have to work because they set up so many other things. Running off-tackle attacks the defense where it often is weakest—at the strongside linebacker. If off-tackle plays are a consistent success, the defense has to weaken its center or flank to compensate.

The sweep takes the off-tackle play a little farther outside. It is aimed around the end, at the outside linebacker, and the defensive back who comes up to force the play. The now predominant 3-4 defense, with its additional linebacker, has made sweeps more difficult to run. Prerequisites to successful execution of the sweep are fast pulling linemen and running backs with enough speed to get outside, turn the corner, and head upfield before the pursuit can react. There are many types of sweeps: the power sweep with both the offensive guards leading the halfback around end; the fullback sweep in which the smaller running back becomes the lead blocker; and the option sweep, in which the running back has the option to run or pass.

THE SWEEP IN ACTION
On a sweep a running back must follow his interference (blockers) around the corner. If he overruns his blockers, he has very little maneuvering room against the sideline. But, if he stays with his blockers into the secondary, he can burst out from behind them into the open.

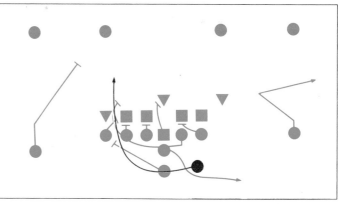

OFF-TACKLE SLANT:
One of pro football's bread-and-butter plays, the off-tackle slant can be run to the strongside (diagram, right) and, with the fullback, to the weakside.

Strongside/Weakside

Pro football teams generally run toward their strength, and their strength is the side with the extra blocking potential of the tight end. The tight end's block, coupled with those of pulling linemen and the lead back, can often be the difference in turning the corner on a sweep or getting by the defensive end on an off-tackle play. When running to the strongside, teams can use their smaller, faster backs because of the extra blocking power available up front.

Running away from the tight end, to the weakside, presents unique offensive problems. The rise of the 3-4 defense, and the outlawing of the crackback block (see page 110), have combined to complicate weakside running. Without the availablity of the tight end as a blocker, everyone else's blocks take on increased significance. In the play diagrammed below right, the running back's block on the linebacker is critical to the success of the play. If the same play were run to the strongside, the linebacker would be the tight end's responsibility. Offenses can generally compensate for the lack of blocking strength on the weakside in two ways. They can run the weakside with their biggest back. Or they can run a two-tight end offense, replacing a wide receiver with a second tight end (see page 40). The second tight end eliminates the strongside-weakside distinction; plays can be run either right or left with equal blocking power.

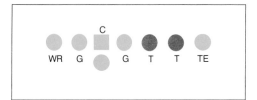

UNBALANCED LINE: A lineman is shifted to overload one side of the offensive formation.

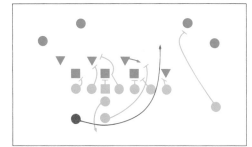

UNBALANCED OFF-TACKLE: The fullback leads the halfback inside the unbalanced tackle.

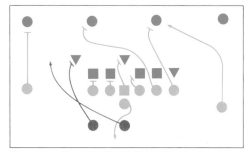

FULLBACK TO THE WEAKSIDE: The halfback clears the way for the fullback around the weakside.

THE UNBALANCED LINE

*To make the strongside even stronger, some teams have revived the **unbalanced line.** When an offensive line is unbalanced, there are three linemen to one side of the center instead of the usual two. (In the play, middle left, the left tackle has been shifted to the right side.) This makes for a formidable armada of blockers on the unbalanced side. Guards also can be shifted to unbalance a line, but the bigger, stronger tackles are shifted more often.*

Bill Walsh on the Unbalanced Line:
"When you confront a defense with an unbalanced line, it has to decide whether to shift its line with your line, or to simply adjust the linebackers. If they fail to adjust, or if they overcompensate, you often can gain a distinct advantage. Even if the defense does slide its linemen, those men are in positions unfamiliar to them. On the other hand, the offensive line isn't used to blocking these new combinations, either. And, there's no way to predict if, or how, the defense will shift and whether they won't move into positions more difficult to block. The unbalanced line is not a panacea—but it is another tool to use to take advantage of the opposition's defense."

Using Motion

Putting a man in motion can do a number of things: 1) It can place a running back closer to the outside before the play begins. From there he can take a quick pitchout or flare pass, or can serve as a lead blocker; 2) It can bring a receiver into the backfield in time to make him a potential ball carrier on end around plays or reverses (see page 33); 3) It can put a receiver, particularly the tight end, in position behind the offensive line to be a lead blocker for a running back; and 4) It can bring a second, third, or fourth player to one side of the formation to serve as blockers or to help flood that side of the field with potential pass receivers. Above all, motion is used to force the defense to make adjustments. By taking advantage of these adjustments, the offense can run to the defense's exposed weak spot.

Sid Gillman on Motion:
"Every team has certain favorite formations. Either the team lines up in those formations, or it can move to them from a different formation before the snap. Sometimes motion is simply a device to keep the defense guessing before the snap, or a method to enable the quarterback to make the defense tip its hand about its coverages. But more and more, when a team uses motion, it is very likely a meaningful part of the play."

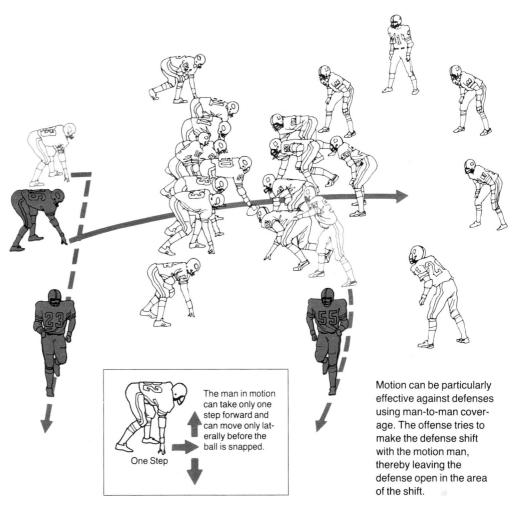

The man in motion can take only one step forward and can move only laterally before the ball is snapped.

One Step

Motion can be particularly effective against defenses using man-to-man coverage. The offense tries to make the defense shift with the motion man, thereby leaving the defense open in the area of the shift.

Draws and Misdirection

The action of the draw play, and its counterpart the screen pass (see pages 46-47), *encourages* big pass rushes. On draw plays, all 11 offensive players behave as if a pass is in the works. At the snap, the linemen assume pass blocking positions, the quarterback drops back, the receivers run their routes downfield, and the running backs assume pass protection blocking positions.

Then the play turns into a run.

The movement of the offensive linemen may be the biggest key to making a draw play work. They must be very convincing as they set up to pass block, so convincing that the defensive linemen will disregard their run responsibilities and rush across the line. Once these defenders have been lured into the backfield, the offensive linemen pick them up (each blocker or combination of blockers takes a defender and tries to force him away from the running area). The quarterback then hands the ball to one of the running backs, who shoots through the hole vacated by the out of position defenders.

If draws and screen passes are used successfully often enough in a game, the defense will be forced to slow its rush so it won't get burned again by the offense's deception. Draw plays by their nature are ideal in obvious passing situations. In such instances, the defense will mount a heavier rush, which makes the rush men more susceptible to the influence blocking of the offensive line.

Another answer to reading and pursuit by the defense is the misdirection play. A misdirection play goes in the wrong direction—wrong according to the action that it shows the defense. The flow of the running backs appears to be heading toward one point of attack, but then suddenly it hits an altogether different one.

With misdirection the offense is trying to freeze and confuse the defensive linemen, at the same time it is trying to force the linebackers to move. Once the linebackers commit to pursuing the initial action of a misdirection play, it is usually too late for them to get back into position before the running back is past. Thus, misdirection plays work well against defenses that have a tendency to flow in one direction.

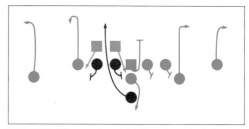

DRAW PLAY: On this quick-hitting draw, the left guard and tackle indicate pass, then split the rushing end and tackle to create a running lane.

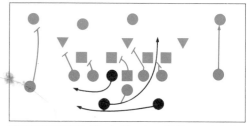

MISDIRECTION: The halfback and left guard start from right to left, but the fullback, instead, takes the ball inside.

Traps

If misdirection is deceptive movement by running backs, traps (another form of influence blocking) entail deceptive movement by linemen. On a trap play, the offensive lineman nearest the hole objective pulls away at the snap, exposing the defensive lineman or linebacker directly over him. That isolated defender then is influenced into the vacated hole and is immediately hit by an offensive lineman pulling from the other side of the formation.

There are tackle traps (with the tackle executing the trap block) and center traps, but the guards are most often called upon to trap defenders. Short traps are run against defensive tackles; long traps are run against defensive ends or linebackers.

There also are false traps (or sucker traps) run against defensive linemen who are quick to read the flow of the play and leave their positions. In the most widely used meaning, a false trap involves pulling a blocker, as on a sweep or trap, thus causing the targeted defensive lineman to misread the play and follow the blocker, leaving his position vacant to be run through by the ball carrier.

No matter what type of trap or false trap is run, though, the key to the success of the play is the quickness, timing, and coordination of the offensive linemen.

NFL teams use misdirection plays, traps, and influence blocking to make basic blocking easier and more effective. When the defense begins to hesitate and read to detect offensive deceptions, it becomes a prime target for ordinary straight-ahead blocks.

A TRAP IN ACTION

1. The right guard slants into the right defensive end, exposing the defensive tackle (75). The left guard (61) pulls behind the center, who takes on the other defensive tackle.

2. The uncovered defensive tackle moves across the line into the trap area and, as the quarterback hands off, is hit by the pulling left guard.

3. The running back makes his cut off the trap block. The right tackle slants into the middle linebacker (58), clearing a running lane into the secondary.

31

At the Goal Line

The basic NFL running game doesn't change much until the offense gets inside the 5 yard line. Then, the offense must alter its running plays to counteract changes the defense always makes close to its own goal line. In a goal line situation, most defenses bring in extra linemen to stop short yardage touchdown thrusts. Offenses respond to these additional defensive linemen by bringing in more "horses" of their own, usually an extra tight end (and sometimes two) and their biggest or most powerful running backs.

Teams prepare and practice offenses for special short-yardage or goal line situations. One problem with many goal line offenses, though, is that teams often become conservative once they are near scoring territory. In essence, they narrow the field to the area between their two tackles and keep plays simple. This not only limits the offense, but it allows the defense more chances to clog holes and stack up the closely spaced blockers. Recently, there has been a move toward a more wide-open philosophy for goal line offense, mirroring the more wide-open approach to the game in general.

GOAL LINE OFFENSE

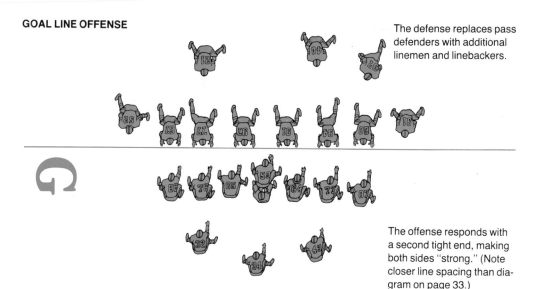

The defense replaces pass defenders with additional linemen and linebackers.

The offense responds with a second tight end, making both sides "strong." (Note closer line spacing than diagram on page 33.)

QUARTERBACK KEEPER

Close to the end zone, defenses go all out to protect the middle of the line against diving running backs and quarterback sneaks. This may weaken them against quick outside runs and passes. Here, the quarterback fakes a handoff to the fullback up the middle to draw the defense in, then "rolls out" (or "bootlegs") left behind the pulling left guard and sprints into the end zone. This "keeper" play could easily become an option pass if a receiver is wide open in the end zone.

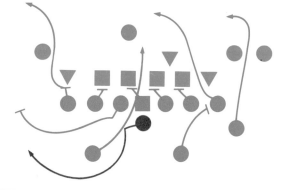

Gadget Plays

All offenses have trick plays up their sleeves. Some are designed especially to work against a certain team, or certain personnel, or certain alignments. But they all come under the heading "razzle-dazzle" and are used sparingly, if at all.

These trick plays are called gadget plays, and a team practices them and keeps them in its playbook just in case. Most trick plays are not spur-of-the-moment calls; they are set up in advance. Just as false traps are set up by guard or tackle traps, running gadget plays, such as reverses, are set up by misdirection and influence blocks.

Reverses are the most common running gadget plays. There is the basic reverse, the double reverse, and the triple reverse—plus option passes from each. On a reverse play, the quarterback runs (sprints out) in one direction and hands the ball off to a running back or receiver going by in the other direction. A double reverse begins the same way, but the first running back or receiver makes a second handoff, making the play change direction a second time. A triple reverse adds yet another handoff.

A variation of the reverse is the end around. Instead of handing off to a running back, the quarterback gives the ball to a wide receiver or tight end who has gone in motion. The receiver takes the ball and sweeps around end, or, if further sleight-of-hand is

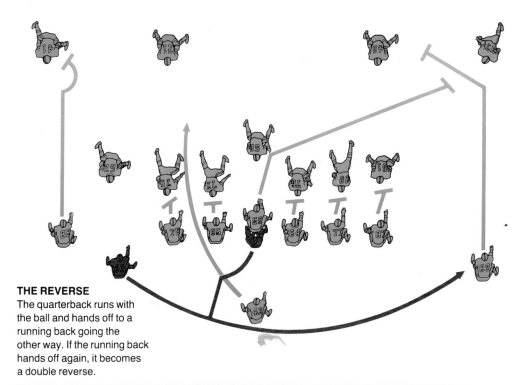

THE REVERSE
The quarterback runs with the ball and hands off to a running back going the other way. If the running back hands off again, it becomes a double reverse.

called for, hands off to a running back.

It is easy to imagine how well-run, well-timed, precisely executed plays of this nature can give a defense fits. It also is easy to see why these plays are such rarities, saved for special situations. First, gadget plays can be slow to develop, giving the defense time to recover from its initial confusion and surprise.

Second, if the defense diagnoses a gadget play correctly, it can result in a substantial loss of yardage for the offense because the main action of the play takes place deep in the backfield. And third, all the ball handling involved in such plays as reverses significantly increases the possibilities of a fumble.

But when gadgets work, they can work big!

Passing

Quarterbacks

It is virtually impossible for a football team to achieve any consistent success without an outstanding quarterback. The entire offense revolves around his performance; he establishes the rhythm and sets the tempo.

Playing quarterback in the NFL can mean a quick ride to glory, but it also is a complex, demanding position, filled with pressures, that requires a uniquely skilled athlete. A quarterback must have a strong arm and a quick release; he has to be able to unload the ball rapidly, with precision, to a very small (but often crowded) point on the field. Overall quickness and durability are important. It also helps to have good size in order to withstand punishing hits, as well as be tall enough to see over huge linemen.

An effective quarterback must possess a number of important intangible qualities as well; he must be an outstanding leader, he must be intelligent, and he needs an ordered, disciplined mind. Also, he needs a sense of timing and patience. The quarterback has to sit back in the pocket and wait for the play to develop. But every fraction of a second that a quarterback "buys" for his receivers by waiting for them to get open on their pass routes increases his own chances of being sacked

> **Walsh on the Quarterback:**
> *"Quarterbacks have to be bright. They have to have instinctive awareness, and they must keep a clear head under stress. The quarterback also has to be able to handle unexpected circumstances. He can't act out of rage or desperation."*

by the defense. It all takes enormous concentration (not to mention courage).

Quarterbacks generally are classed as either scramblers or pocket passers, depending on their style of play and their mobility. Scrambling and pocket quarterbacks both must be outstanding passers. But the scramblers often run with the ball—particularly when their original plays break down—and

are adept at passing on the run.

The passing game in the NFL today, however, is predicated on pocket passing, in which the quarterback will retreat into the pocket, set up, and quickly study his options. Mobility is still an asset, of course; it helps a quarterback to be an escape artist when a defensive lineman is breathing down his neck. Many quarterbacks who were scramblers and runners early in their careers become pocket passers as age and injuries take their toll.

Ultimately, the success or failure of a passing game hinges on a quarterback's ability to read the defensive coverage. If a quarterback senses before the snap that the play called in the huddle won't work against the defensive alignment he sees at the line of scrimmage, it is up to him to call an audible, switching to a play that has a better chance of success against that particular coverage.

There are 11 men on an offensive unit, each with an important role. But it is the quarterback who is relied upon to have the instincts and the intelligence to outwit the defense.

> **Bart Starr on the Quarterback:**
> *"The quarterback has to have the highest boiling point on the team. He must be cool. He has to be able to concentrate on fundamentals and techniques. The way the quarterback can retaliate is by performing and executing well."*

Pass Blocking

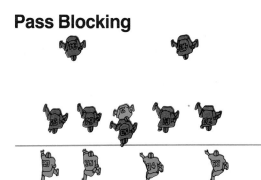

1. When pass blocking, the offensive linemen don't fire out at the men over them, as they would if the play was a run.

2. Instead, as the quarterback begins his drop, the linemen step back off the line, warding off the pass rushers.

3. The linemen form a pocket like a fence around the quarterback; the backs pick up defenders who break through.

Quarterback may be the spotlight position in the NFL, but a quarterback will be in little position for glamor if his pass protection fails.

Good blocking probably is even more important to the success of the passing attack than it is to the running game.

There is one basic distinction between run blocking and pass blocking. Instead of firing across the line of scrimmage to clear defenders out of the path of a ball carrier, pass blocking usually requires offensive linemen to retreat one-to-three steps from the line when the ball is snapped, set up and brace for impact, and then ward off the hard-charging defensive players coming into the backfield.

Until recently, the blocker operated at a disadvantage. Under NFL rules, his hands had to be cupped or closed, and his arms had to be "flexed" inward—they could not be extended forward to create a push.

But following the 1977 season the rules were relaxed, allowing the blocker to extend his arms and open his hands—an amendment that swung the advantage full circle to the offense.

Now, after breaking a pass rusher's momentum with an initial strike, a blocker can fend him off with open hands, keeping him at bay with open arms.

The key to pass blocking always is positioning. The blocker has to face his man, with his shoulders square and his head up, never taking his eye off his target.

Size and strength are the raw materials for an offensive lineman, and so are feet. The best linemen all have "quick feet", meaning they can dance agilely, like a boxer. They can slide from side to side, pedal back and forth, or swivel from angle to angle, all while maintaining unshakeable balance.

In addition to the offensive linemen, running backs also are called upon to pass block. The general rule for blocking assignments is to try to keep the offensive linemen matched against the defensive linemen, and the running backs matched against any charging linebackers or defensive backs.

The pass protectors know they have usually done their job well if they have kept the pass rush away from the quarterback for at least 2.5 seconds, because that is usually all the time a quarterback needs to get his pass away.

Pass Receivers

Offensive formations are primarily dictated by the positioning of the wide receivers, tight ends, and running backs, all of whom are eligible to catch passes on every play.

Wide receivers are so designated because they usually are split away from the interior linemen. In most normal formations, there will be two wide receivers, one split to the left and one split to the right.

Wide receivers are part sprinter and part acrobat; they must have the speed to beat a defender and the ability to catch the ball in a crowd. Since they usually have slighter builds than the rest of the offensive personnel, they

aren't called upon to block as much as the linemen and running backs. (Of course, when they do—usually downfield—theirs may be the final block to spring a ball carrier free for a touchdown.) Wide receivers who are not the primary targets in a passing play are used as decoys.

The tight end lines up close to one of the two offensive tackles. Because tight ends (on the average) are much more physically imposing than wide receivers, they present a different set of problems for the defense. The tight end is constantly used to block on running and passing plays, and also has become an increasingly attractive passing target.

Running backs also are being used more fre-

There is an unspoken communication between a quarterback and his receiver. Each has an instinctive awareness of what to expect in a given situation.

In addition to speed, quickness, and good hands, a receiver must have the ability to concentrate totally on the ball, to "look" the ball into his hands— even with tacklers descending upon him.

quently as receivers. They always have been integrated into pass blocking schemes, and always have been available for pass catching duty. But more than ever there is a demand for running backs who can catch the ball.

GAME TRENDS

EVOLUTION OF THE TIGHT END

As the passing game has assumed more importance in pro football, so has the tight end. Against the nickel (and dime) defenses and zones that feature double coverage of wide receivers, it is the tight end who will often find himself matched against single coverage. Instead of the big, lumbering tight ends of a decade ago, who were thought of (and often used) as little more than auxiliary tackles, a new breed of sleeker tight ends is emerging, with the strength to battle linebackers head-on, the speed to go on deep pass routes, and the hands to hold onto difficult passes. Instead of being a blocker who is used as a receiver only as an element of surprise, the prototypic tight end in today's game is sometimes thought of as "a big wide receiver."

Consequently, the use of multiple tight ends in passing formations has gained prominence. The presence of an extra tight end on the line of scrimmage in effect gives the offense two strongsides, and can provide an effective way to attack a light linebacker who ordinarily plays (or rotates to) the weakside away from the tight end.

Pass Patterns

All receivers run patterns, or routes, to break free from defenders and get open. There are different distance options that can be utilized on nearly every pass route, and receivers spend hours perfecting their fakes, cuts, and timing so that their patterns become disciplined and sharp. Receivers also synchronize their routes with the quarterback so he instinctively will know where the receiver is throughout the pass pattern and how to time his release.

Obviously, different pass patterns are required for running backs, wide receivers, and tight ends. When the proper complementary patterns are blended with sound blocking schemes, the passing game can become an artistic success, as well as an effective means to an end.

Receivers also play an important part on running plays; they usually try to run convincing pass patterns to draw attention—and defenders—away from the direction of the run.

Through their flare action (the coordinated movement of the running backs as they block or go out for passes), running backs often hold the keys to passing plays.

It is impossible to run a perfect pattern every time. Bad field conditions, inclement weather, congestion caused by the defense, and even a slip can play havoc with a receiver's pattern. When a pattern is irrevocably broken, the receiver will try to improvise a new route in an attempt to get open.

THE PASSING TREE

Every pass pattern in a team's offense is part of a larger series, which, when drawn on a blackboard, can resemble a leafless tree, with every branch a pass route. In a game there would be even more turns and angles on each pattern to reflect the "moves" a receiver employs to elude pass defenders.

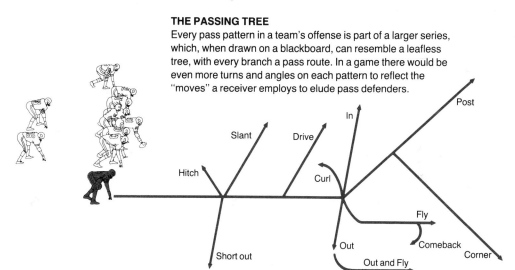

RUNNING BACK ROUTES

Because running backs begin their pass routes several steps behind the line of scrimmage, their assortment of pass patterns differs slightly from those of wide receivers and tight ends. The chart at right displays some of the most frequently used pass patterns for running backs. (The names of the patterns differ from team to team, but usually the designation of a pass pattern describes the route.)

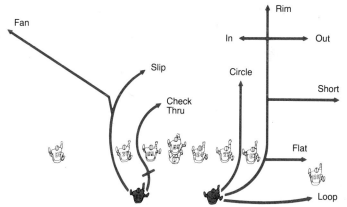

Short Passing Game

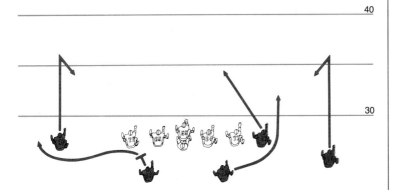

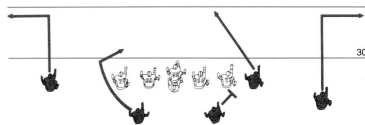

Both wide receivers turn in after a quick burst off the line as the tight end angles across the middle. The running backs act as safety valve receivers.

While the two wide receivers run out patterns toward the sidelines, the tight end and one running back go over the middle. The other back blocks.

For a team that does not have a great running back, an offense structured around a short passing game can be the surest way to control the ball.

The short, ball control passing game requires patience above all. It also demands more discipline and even tighter execution than the running game (because of the more intricate timing involved).

But the rewards can be greater. Instead of averaging 3.5 or 4.0 yards per rush (as most NFL teams do), a team that can sustain a successful short passing game can average up to 7 or 8 yards per completion.

The success of the short passing game is based in large part on an ability to quickly scatter the linebackers (especially against a 3-4 defense). One way offenses try to do this is to greatly vary their formations with motion (see pages 42-43) and shifts before the snap to confuse the coverage.

It is crucial for receivers to get off the line of scrimmage quickly. Although defenders can no longer jostle receivers all over the field before the ball is thrown, they still can "chuck" (bump) the receiver once as long as it's done within five yards of the line of scrimmage.

The receiver, therefore, must have outstanding release technique so he can maintain his pattern and break loose despite any initial contact from a linebacker or defensive back.

The use of delay patterns, screen passes (see page 46), quick passes over the middle to the tight end, pick plays (where a receiver actually sets a screen for another receiver downfield), and pass routes that attack the spots underneath the deep coverage area of a zone defense all are important methods of establishing a short passing game.

Long Passing Game

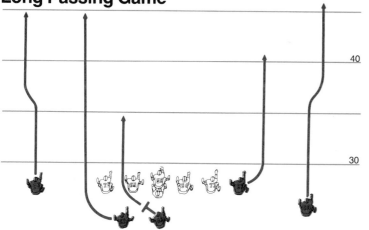

If the wide receiver on the deep pattern is in trouble, the quarterback has several other passing options, including the two running backs.

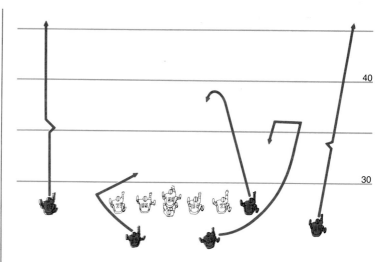

The tight end and both running backs flood the middle as the two wide receivers streak down the sidelines.

The most exciting play in pro football is the long pass—"the bomb." It is the quickest way to put six points on the scoreboard.

Not coincidentally, the bomb also is probably the hardest play to execute consistently, both because of the many defenses designed to stop it and the timing that is required—from the quarterback getting the time to set, find his receiver, and throw; to the receiver beating the initial chuck, getting open, and making the catch.

The objective of the long passing game is to isolate one or more receivers deep downfield against just one defender. That means the rest of the play must be designed to attract the attention of the defense away from the deep receiver(s).

Wide receivers always have been the most frequent targets for long passes because of their great speed and elusive moves. But as the passing game has opened up, running backs and tight ends also are increasingly being called on to run long pass routes.

There are some obvious downs and situations that call for a long pass. If a team is faced with a third-and-30 situation, it's a safe bet it isn't going to run up the middle very often.

But because defenses adjust to such situations with extra men in the secondary (or extra pass rushers), the bomb is an even more effective weapon when it is tried under less obvious circumstances, such as third-and-inches, or even first-and-10.

It a team can establish early success at throwing long, it can soften up the defense, and make it even more vulnerable to the other two major prongs in its offensive attack—the short pass and the running game.

Multiple Receiver Formations

Because the refinement of the passing game has made passing an increasingly high-percentage play, coaches always are looking for new formations and plays.

For some time they have tried three and even four wide receivers on passing downs, substituting for slower tight ends and blocking backs. Some teams even have cultivated running backs as passing play specialists, bringing them in for critical passing situations.

The use of so many different offensive "looks" by some teams has made it more difficult to make a distinction between "normal" and "radical" formations. The rule is becoming clearer and clearer: anything goes—double- and triple-wing formations (with two or three wide receivers set to one side of the ball); Shotgun formations (see page 45); no running backs in the backfield; double and triple tight end formations. All of those—and more—are used more frequently, and effectively, than ever before.

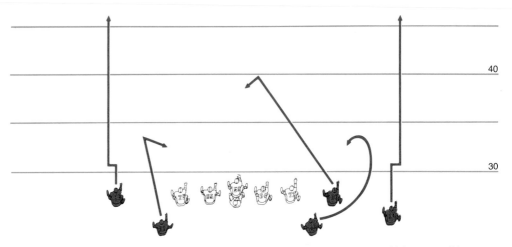

The spread offense is designed to do just that—spread the defensive coverage as widely as possible. Five receivers disperse into different areas to reduce potential for double coverage.

Joe Gibbs on Multiple Receivers:
"You start with the ambition of avoiding the two things that kill off the passing game: the sack and the interception. One way to accomplish that is to place your receivers all over the field and have a quarterback with a quick release so well instructed in reading defenses that he always throws into the thinnest part of the coverage. Every pass should have a built-in big play. Why settle for a twelve-yard gain if there is a fifty-yard gain possible? Multiple receivers give you the flexibility to go for broke on every play."

GAME TRENDS

THE SPREAD OFFENSE
One of the best ways an offense can stretch a defense is to use a spread formation, stationing three receivers on one side of the ball and two on the opposite side—with nobody but the quarterback in the backfield. One obvious advantage of the spread is that it can deliver five receivers into the secondary very quickly. The quarterback must get rid of the ball just as quickly, because he is stranded with no backfield blockers. In the event one or more linebackers blitz against a spread, the quarterback should be able to locate a hot (uncovered) receiver in the short zone area.

Stretching the Defense

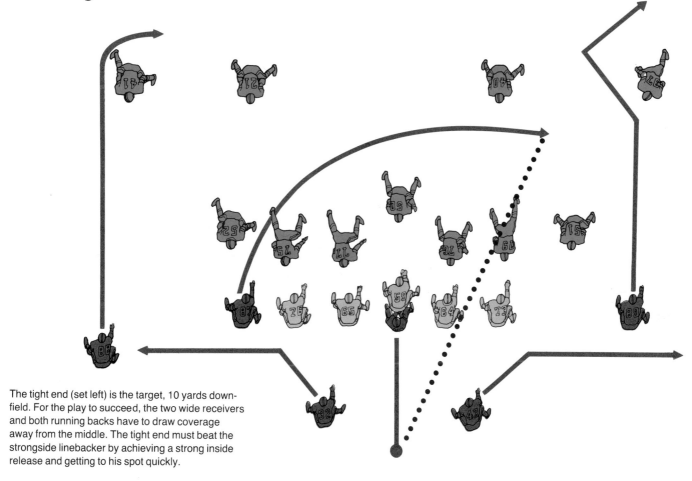

The tight end (set left) is the target, 10 yards downfield. For the play to succeed, the two wide receivers and both running backs have to draw coverage away from the middle. The tight end must beat the strongside linebacker by achieving a strong inside release and getting to his spot quickly.

Motion

Using motion can be an important part of passing strategy because it can cause imbalances and mismatches that favor the offense. Also, by reading how a defense reacts or adjusts to motion, a quarterback often can determine what type of defense has been called for that play. A quarterback can't read an entire defense, but how a cornerback or safety reacts to a halfback in motion can be one indicator of zone or man-to-man coverage.

Against a 3-4 defense, a tight end shift can potentially pull as many as six people (the two safeties and all four linebackers) out of position, forcing them to rearrange their defensive alignment the instant prior to the snap of the ball, which increases the chance for confusion.

Sometimes motion is simply window dressing. It won't affect the flow of the play, but is done merely to keep the defense on edge, to give it something extra to think about, such as three receivers on one side of the field.

A zone defense won't always react to motion, which can negate its tactical effect *if* the motion is only a ploy. However, if there is no adjustment or rotation by the defense, it might be caught badly off balance, facing a formidable strongside assault with a weakside formation.

EVOLUTION OF A PLAY

1. The backs and receivers break from the huddle and line up: the tight end is split several steps wide to the left and both running backs are set to the strongside.

2. Both backs shift, with the fullback setting up behind the quarterback and the halfback moving to the weakside. The tight end moves closer to the left tackle.

3. A wide receiver goes into motion, splitting wide to the left and settles (just beyond the area originally occupied by the halfback) before the snap of the ball.

4. Finally, after all of the pre-snap motion, the formation is set. The play is a fullback sweep, with the right guard pulling to lead the blocking.

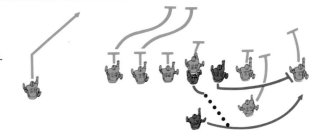

Motion in Action

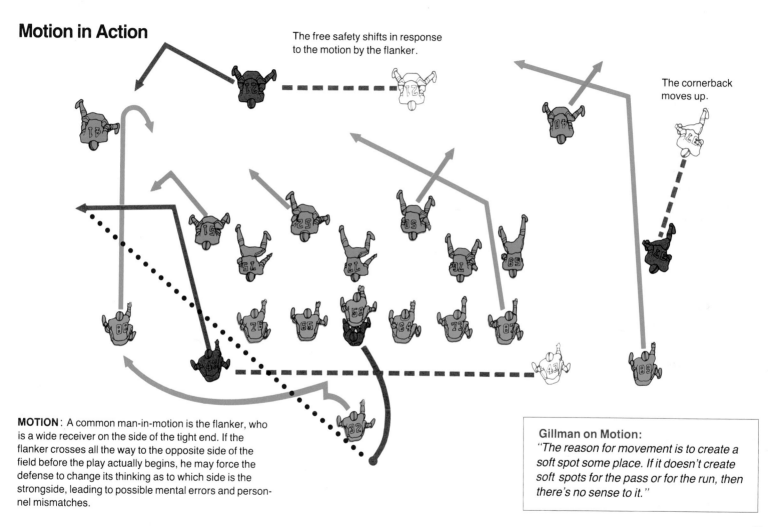

The free safety shifts in response to the motion by the flanker.

The cornerback moves up.

MOTION: A common man-in-motion is the flanker, who is a wide receiver on the side of the tight end. If the flanker crosses all the way to the opposite side of the field before the play actually begins, he may force the defense to change its thinking as to which side is the strongside, leading to possible mental errors and personnel mismatches.

Gillman on Motion:
"The reason for movement is to create a soft spot some place. If it doesn't create soft spots for the pass or for the run, then there's no sense to it."

43

Play Action Passes

1. At the snap the quarterback spins around toward the running back for an apparent handoff or pitch.

2. As the offensive linemen initiate their blocks to create a hole, the quarterback makes his fake to a running back.

3. The back hits the hole (without the ball) and continues through, as the quarterback rolls out to the left in search of a receiver.

One of the most popular methods of keeping linebackers off balance is the play action pass.

Essentially, the play action pass is a pass off a fake run. Like its opposite the draw play (a run off a fake pass), in order for it to work, the play fake has to be pulled off expertly; it has to be believable. The offensive linemen must appear to be blocking for a running play, by pulling and giving the appearance of leading a sweep, for instance, while the quarterback fakes a handoff to a running back who continues through the line.

If the linebackers have been properly fooled by this deception, and are pulled into the line of scrimmage area expecting a run, some of the short zones will be vacant. And that is where the quarterback throws, often to a running back who has delayed a moment in the backfield before slipping out on his pass route.

Play action is a strategy that is largely dictated by down and distance. It seldom works on obvious passing downs because the linebackers won't go for the run fake as readily. But it is a play that can work beautifully on third-and-inches or first-and-10. It is also a prevalent part of the goal line passing game, when the defense is constantly on the lookout for the run.

The value of a successful play action pass lies not only in whatever yardage it reaps, but also in its ability to help open up the running attack. It is an extremely useful strategy if the defense has previously been successful in shutting down running plays.

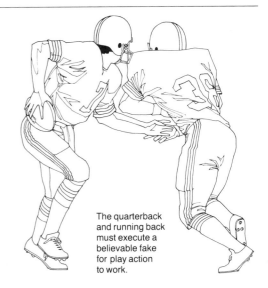

The quarterback and running back must execute a believable fake for play action to work.

The Shotgun

Bud Grant on the Shotgun:
"What the Shotgun does is give us maybe a fraction of a second of extra time with the ball to look at the coverage, look at the receivers, see the rush, and get rid of the ball."

One way to reduce the initiative of special defenses that are designed to sabotage the passing game—even if the offense still has to pass—is to use the Shotgun formation. In the Shotgun, the quarterback lines up five or six yards behind the center, or drops back to a similar spot before the ball is snapped.

Probably the biggest advantage of the Shotgun is that it enhances the quarterback's ability to read the defensive coverage. Because he is already in position to pass, with the field in front of him, the quarterback has a panoramic view of the defense.

The Shotgun has gained in popularity during the past few years, partly as an answer to defenses featuring extra pass defenders.

Ray Perkins on the Shotgun:
"It's not so much that the quarterback has longer to get off his pass, it's just that he's seeing the defense longer. That means he should be able to execute the play a little more quickly."

A typical Shotgun play: The quarterback is isolated and the receivers are spread.

The extra time a quarterback receives by already being in position to pass creates less of a need for backfield blocking.

But not every team uses the Shotgun, due to its inherent disadvantages. The center has to make his long snap "blind" (without looking between his legs), because he has to handle his blocking assignment (the nose tackle in the 3-4, or a dogging middle linebacker in the 4-3). That increases the chance of a miscue on the exchange—particularly in bad weather. Also, crowd noise can interfere with the quarterback's signal call. And, finally, though there are running plays from the Shotgun formation, they are used infrequently.

When a team goes into a Shotgun any of the surprise factor is lost. The defense can be almost certain the play is a pass.

Tom Landry on the Spread (Shotgun):
"If the other team uses a deliberate pass defense, why shouldn't we use a deliberate pass offense? We figure it [the Shotgun] buys the quarterback a second-and-a-half more of reading time before the rush can get to him."

Screen Passes

An effective strategy against a defense mounting a heavy pass rush is the use of the screen pass.

On a typical screen, as the quarterback drops into position to throw, the offensive linemen relax their blocks slightly to allow a little penetration by the defense into the backfield. As the defensive rush men charge by, the offensive linemen slide off in the direction of the intended pass.

Meanwhile, a wide receiver steps back off the line of scrimmage, or a running back swings into the flat. The quarterback, sometimes after a fake arm pump to enhance the impression that the play is going to be a down-

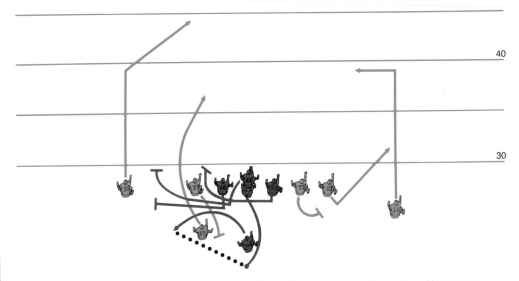

On this screen, the strongside running back moves to the weakside to become the receiver. He goes *underneath* the rush of the defensive end on that side. His screen is comprised of guards and the center.

Gillman on the Screen Pass:

"The most popular pass in pro football today is the option screen pass. It has brought the screen pass back into vogue. The advantage of the play is that a receiver will run a quick pattern, usually about fifteen yards, that is timed exactly with the drop of the quarterback. The quarterback has the option of throwing to that receiver downfield for a positive gain. However, if the receiver is covered, the quarterback will have a wall [of blockers] assembled in front of him, and at that point he can still unload a pass to the screen man."

---

field pass, then will loop a pass over the oncoming rushers to the waiting receiver behind the line, who by then has a wall of blockers in front of him comprised of the regrouped offensive linemen. (Screens are one of the few occasions when a center will pull from his original position to lead the blocking.)

Screens can work particularly well against zone defenses, because the linebackers often will have run off from their areas to cover the faked deep pass and will be out of position to cover the receiver or back running the shorter screen route.

One of the advantages of the screen pass is that it can create additional running room for quick backs who may have had trouble breaking loose on ordinary runs from scrimmage.

But in order to make screens more effective, a team usually has to establish a successful passing game, which in turn inspires a hard pass rush by the defense (including blitzes, which can leave a defense particularly vulnerable to screens).

Option Screen Pass in Action

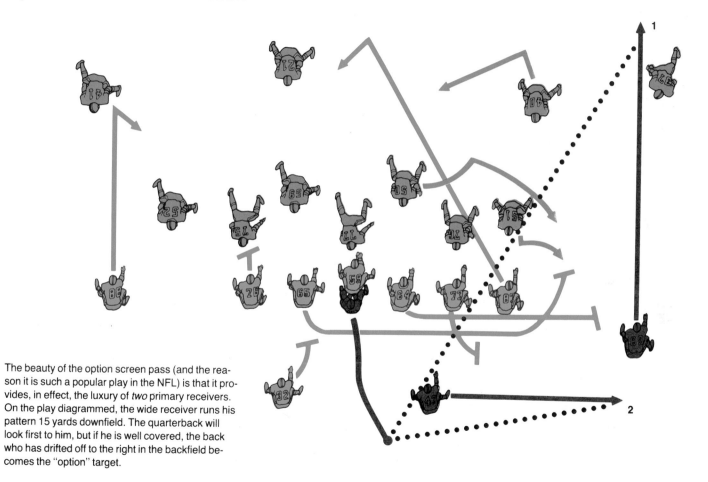

The beauty of the option screen pass (and the reason it is such a popular play in the NFL) is that it provides, in effect, the luxury of *two* primary receivers. On the play diagrammed, the wide receiver runs his pattern 15 yards downfield. The quarterback will look first to him, but if he is well covered, the back who has drifted off to the right in the backfield becomes the "option" target.

Option Passing

If a passing play breaks down because all of the designated receivers are covered, a quarterback always has the option of attempting to salvage the play and perhaps pick up yardage by running with the ball. But some plays are specifically designed to give the quarterback, or in some cases a running back, the option either to pass *or* to run. Based on how the defense reacts to the early development of the play, the quarterback or running back makes a split-second decision on which option is likely to net more yardage.

Teams that have running backs who also can pass the ball will always have one or more plays to take advantage of that skill. Once a team has demonstrated that it will use an option pass in a game, it makes the defense contend with one more variable

If an option pass is executed properly, and it catches the defense napping, it often can result in a big gain for the offense. However, it is used sparingly because it is usually a difficult play to execute, the timing can be extremely tricky, and the ball often has to be thrown off balance on the run.

HALFBACK GO MOTION

The halfback goes in motion before the snap. The quarterback fakes a draw up the middle to the fullback, who becomes a blocker. The halfback swings to the outside and takes off on a go pattern (deep). The quarterback rolls right, retaining the option of either (1) passing to the halfback or (2) running behind the pulling left guard.

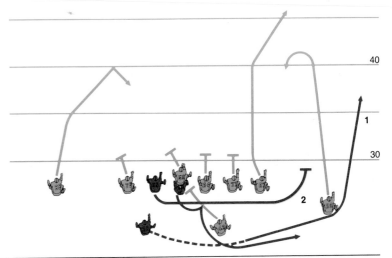

FULLBACK OPTION PASS

This fullback option begins with a lateral toss to the fullback from the quarterback. If the fullback can throw long, he has the option of (1) hitting the flanker on a deep go pattern. Or, (2) he can hit the tight end for a short gain. Or, (3) if the receivers are covered, he can follow the pulling tackle and run with the ball.

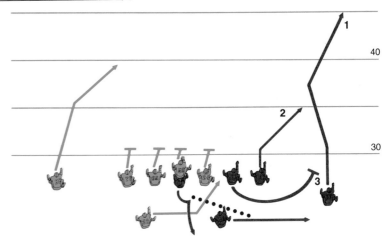

Goal Line Passing Game

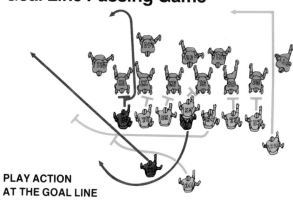

**PLAY ACTION
AT THE GOAL LINE**

Play action passes are often used near the goal line. Here the quarterback fakes to the fullback and rolls out to the left, preparing to pass.

**THE TIGHT END
AT THE GOAL LINE**

The flanker goes in motion and cuts inside right tackle, flooding the middle with the two running backs, hopefully leaving the tight end with single coverage.

Passing strategy—like running strategy—changes once a team moves inside its opponent's 10 yard line. Some teams reduce their number of passing attempts once they approach the end zone, on the theory that because they are so close to a touchdown (or at least a field goal, if they can't actually get in the end zone), they don't want to risk losing

the ball via an interception.

But a growing number of teams are now passing aggressively near the goal line, and there seems to be a consensus on the sound logic for doing so.

When an offense nears the end zone, the deep pass is no longer a threat. Consequently, the defense usually will insert extra linemen and linebackers into the game, replacing the defensive backs who are no longer needed to cover deep.

These additional defenders make it more difficult to run the closer a team gets to its opponent's end zone. Since it is harder to run and because the defense is still looking for the run first, it follows that passing plays can exploit

and get behind a tightly concentrated goal line defensive alignment.

> **Faulkner on Goal Line Passing:**
> *"The latest trend in goal line offenses is to let it [the ball] fly. You've gone ninety yards with the pass, so you might as well use short, low-risk passes to take you the rest of the way."*

> **Walsh on Goal Line Passing:**
> *"The use of extra tight ends in a goal line situation has become a big factor. The tight end is the type of athlete who can block linebackers well. Plus, when the tight end is lined up as a flanker, it gives you real power blocking. And, he still is capable of being a receiver. It's ideal to have the option of using two or even three tight ends on the goal line. So many teams are doing it that it's been proven to be an advantage."*

Passing Gadgets

Flea-flickers, linemen set as wingbacks, and throwback passes to the quarterback are examples of passing gadget plays, which can occur to coaches at three o'clock in the morning, causing them to sit up in bed, take pencil and pad in hand, and diagram an exciting new play for the world.

As you might expect, gadget plays are most effective when least suspected, although teams will rarely attempt an elaborate gadget play deep in their own territory, or near an opponent's goal line.

Gadget plays have been around for a long time. The term flea-flicker, for instance, originated in the 1920s, and was used to describe a play in which a quarterback completed a pass to a receiver downfield, who then lateraled the ball to a trailing receiver for an additional gain. Miami used a beautifully executed flea-flicker play to score a touchdown late in the first half of its 1981 AFC Divisional Playoff Game against San Diego.

Over the years the phrase flea-flicker has been broadened by popular usage to describe a variety of different gadget plays that involve multiple passes and/or laterals.

Although they can be risky maneuvers, gadget plays have frequently been sprung in big games; both Cincinnati and San Francisco successfully used gadget passes in Super Bowl XVI. (The play the 49ers used is shown opposite.)

A different kind of gadget play is the tipped ball pass (above), which also is called a "Hail Mary" or "Big Ben" play. If a team's final gasp for victory is riding on one play, and it is too far away from the end zone to try a run, and it needs more than a field goal, there's only one thing to do. The offense knows it, the defense knows it, and everyone in the stands knows it:

It has to throw a pass up for grabs in the end zone and hope one of its players ends up with the ball.

With the rule change that made it legal for an offensive player to catch a pass first touched by another offensive player, the odds in favor of such a desperation pass working have improved.

Double Reverse Pass

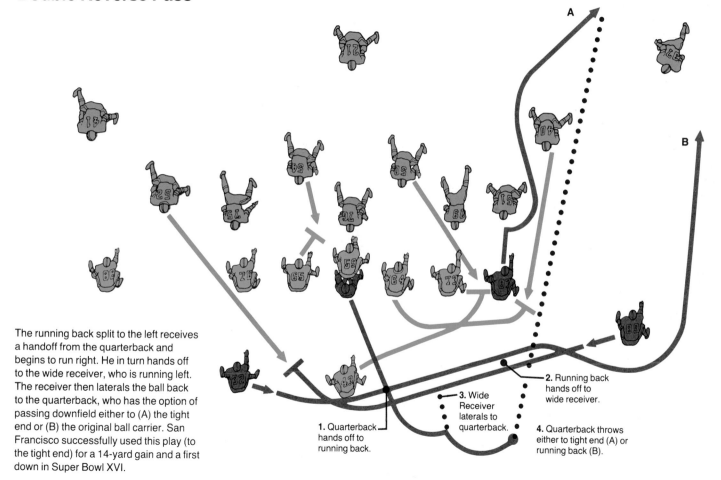

A

B

The running back split to the left receives a handoff from the quarterback and begins to run right. He in turn hands off to the wide receiver, who is running left. The receiver then laterals the ball back to the quarterback, who has the option of passing downfield either to (A) the tight end or (B) the original ball carrier. San Francisco successfully used this play (to the tight end) for a 14-yard gain and a first down in Super Bowl XVI.

1. Quarterback hands off to running back.

2. Running back hands off to wide receiver.

3. Wide Receiver laterals to quarterback.

4. Quarterback throws either to tight end (A) or running back (B).

Defense

3-4 Defense

The 3-4 has become the most prevalent defense in the NFL.

It features a three-man front line made up of a nose tackle (see below) flanked by two defensive ends. The nose tackle sets directly across from the offensive center. The ends play straight across or slightly to either side of the offensive tackles.

The ends must determine in a split second from the offensive tackle's initial thrust whether the play is going to be a run or a pass. Generally, the tackle fires out and attacks the end if the play is a run; he will drop back to block if it's a pass. If the play is a run the defensive end will move toward the play's flow. On a pass he'll rush the quarterback with containment in mind, trying to prevent him from scrambling for a big gain.

The three down linemen (called down be-

Offenses resort extensively to option plays against a 3-4 to cut down the linebackers' mobile pursuit.

In the 3-4, linebackers can "stay home," rush, or drop back to provide extra pass protection.

cause they set up close to the ground in three-point stances before the snap) are supported by four linebackers. The inside linebackers roam the area directly between the two defensive ends. The two outside linebackers set up outside the defensive ends.

The linebackers playing inside are bigger and stronger than the outside men, who rely more on quickness and agility to play their positions. Linebackers in the 3-4 also must have the speed to cover receivers because both inside and outside linebackers have pass coverage responsibilities that vary from play to play depending on type of coverage called.

On runs, the inside linebackers are responsible for cutting off ball carriers who get past the down linemen. The linebackers outside must contain running plays, forcing them inside or stopping them altogether.

In the 3-4, as well as the 4-3 (see opposite page), two cornerbacks and two safeties (free and strong) are set in the secondary. All four provide pass coverage, with the cornerbacks also having significant roles as run defenders.

4-3 Defense

The 4-3 defense was the primary defense used in the NFL in the 1950s, 1960s, and early 1970s. Since the advent of the 3-4, the popularity of the 4-3 has declined, but virtually every team still uses it in certain game situations, such as on sure passing downs.

In the 4-3, two defensive tackles set up directly opposite the offensive guards. Two defensive ends flank the tackles and play head-up, or slightly outside, the offensive tackles.

The 4-3, with its extra defensive lineman, is good against the run because there are more tacklers waiting for the running back at the line of scrimmage and because four defensive front men can better neutralize the blocks of four or five offensive interior linemen.

One way to attack the 4-3 is to use play action passes, making the linebackers commit early.

The middle linebacker is the key to the 4-3; he has the best view of what the offense is doing.

For the same reason—one more lineman—defenses using the 4-3 can generate a much greater pass rush, making it harder for offensive lines to double- and triple-team the individual rush men.

Three linebackers (one middle and two outside) position themselves behind the defensive linemen in the 4-3. The middle linebacker places himself anywhere between the two defensive tackles, similar to the alignment of inside linebackers in the 3-4. The deployment of the outside linebackers is more flexible in the 4-3. One linebacker will always line up on the tight end's side of the formation. The other outside linebacker sets himself on the opposite side of the middle linebacker.

All three linebackers must be very mobile because they are responsible for covering more area than any of the linebackers in the 3-4. To compensate for their large territories, and to confuse the quarterback, the three players will not start each play from the same position. They constantly move around into new areas behind the defensive linemen to support the down linemen and fill the running lanes if a run develops.

The Flex

The Flex defense (so named because it is a "flexible" 4-3) is designed primarily to stop the run. It stalls an option running attack by closing all gaps in the line. However, the Flex is a relatively weak defense against the pass because defensive linemen must read run "keys" first; this cuts down on their ability to rush the passer. In the typical Flex alignment, there are seven men near the line of scrimmage (four down linemen and three linebackers). Two defensive linemen (in any combination) set up two to three yards off the line of scrimmage. The other two linemen position themselves normally and attack the offense. The players off the line are passive, making no penetration. They wait and read, then react to the play.

Defensive Signals

A middle (or inside) linebacker is the quarterback of the defense on most NFL teams, and is responsible for calling the defensive front and coverage formation. He's given this job because he has the best position on the field to see what the offense is doing.

Like his counterpart on offense, the linebacker does not usually select the formations himself. He often gets the defensive play call by looking to a coach on the sideline for a hand signal that dictates what set to use. Or, the defensive coach can send a substitute player into the game with the play. (Though

Because the Flex is a reading, not penetrating, defense, it generates less of a pass rush.

The rules for the offset men in the Flex are basic: Read the play, then react to the ball.

rare, a team can designate a very experienced veteran to choose the signals on the field.)

Once the defensive play is chosen, the middle linebacker turns to his teammates in the huddle and relays the information the coach has given him. He will first call out the defensive front, 4-3 or 3-4, any over or under shifts (see page 63), and if a stunt, stack, and/or pinch (see pages 64-65) are to be used. He then calls the pass coverage, either zone or man-to-man.

The middle linebacker also may audibilize the defensive call at the line of scrimmage based on what offensive formation is shown.

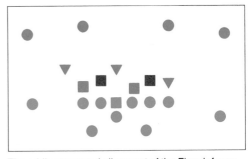

The oddly staggered alignment of the Flex defense gives it a "picket fence" look.

Short Yardage/Goal Line Defense

In some short yardage and most goal line situations, the defense usually will bring in three or four extra linemen, replacing the outside linebackers and one or both safeties. The defensive linemen will set up in the gaps between each offensive player, getting in stances as low to the ground as possible. Their job is to penetrate, undermine the surge of the offense, fill in the holes in the line, and stack the play up.

The middle linebacker often will be the only man set off the line of scrimmage. When the ball is snapped, he instantly tries to recognize where the play is going and propels himself to that point, hopefully meeting the ball carrier head-on and driving him back.

The drawback to bringing in extra defensive linemen is that the defense becomes vulnerable to a play action fake (see page 44) or a pass. Because they are playing without much pass defense support, the cornerbacks and the safeties (if they're in the game), have to be alert to running backs coming out of the backfield as receivers, or receivers slipping off the line into the end zone unnoticed.

If the defense is concentrated in the middle, the quarterback may try a play action fake and option pass.

The defense generally will bring in extra linemen in goal line situations, but does so at the expense of pass coverage.

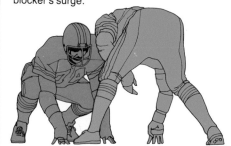

On short yardage plays, defensive linemen assume low stances to "submarine" a blocker's surge.

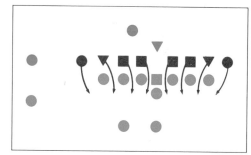

The defense's assignment at the goal line is to fill all the gaps and stack up the play.

57

Strongside/Weakside

Just as on offense, the strongside and weak-side of a defense are determined by the positioning of the tight end. Whichever side of the offensive formation the tight end sets up on also becomes the strongside of the defense. If the tight end goes in motion or shifts sides, the strongside designation goes with him.

The defense, no matter whether it is in a 3-4 or 4-3 alignment, has one outside line-backer who always positions himself to the tight end's side of the field. This is the strong-side linebacker. The opposite linebacker is designated weakside.

In the defensive secondary, the way both safeties line up also is determined by the positioning of the tight end. The strong safety goes to the strongside of the defense, while the free (or weak) safety plays on the other side and is allowed to roam, his man technically being the quarterback.

Weakside
linebacker

Free
(or weak)
safety

Strong
safety

Tight
end

Strongside
linebacker

The defense positions itself according to where the tight end lines up in the offensive formation. If the offense sends the tight end in motion, thus reversing the strong and weak sides of the formation, the defense must adjust immediately or risk leaving itself vulnerable on the original weakside.

Adjusting to Motion

When the offense sends a man in motion, the defense has to adjust, because motion can change the strength of the offensive formation from one side to the other. The adjustments a team makes depend entirely on its defensive personnel.

Teams that are strong in man-to-man coverage (see page 72) react quickly to changes in strength. They send a defensive player across the field (right, above) following the motion man. The defense then compensates to the side away from the motion, to protect from being left open in the area vacated by the man following the motion.

The defense also can rotate to or away from the motion (right, below). These adjustments occur when the defense is playing a zone coverage (see page 70). In this case, when an offensive player goes in motion, the defense (linebackers and defensive backs) doesn't follow him. Instead, the players rotate at the snap of the ball to their predetermined areas of assignment.

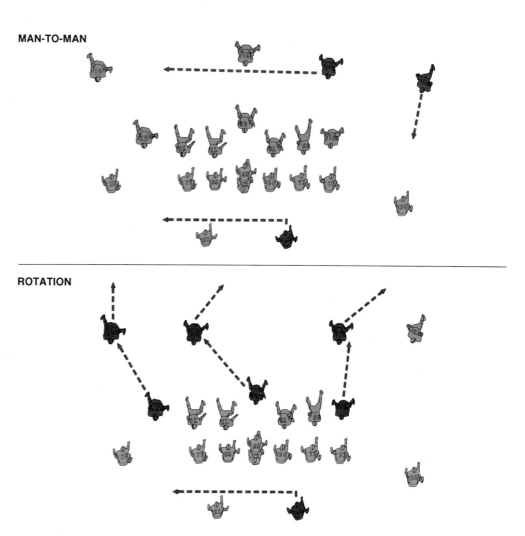

MAN-TO-MAN

ROTATION

Defensive Keys

Keys help defensive players anticipate what type of play the offensive team is going to run. Each player on defense has a mental checklist to go through before each play. He must key (watch) areas of the field and certain offensive players immediately before and after the ball is snapped. In a split second, by reading his keys, he has to determine whether the play is a run or pass. He then instinctively reacts to his keys and assumes his defensive role given the front or formation his team is in. Keys aren't always reliable, though. Many times an offense will show false keys to deceive the defense.

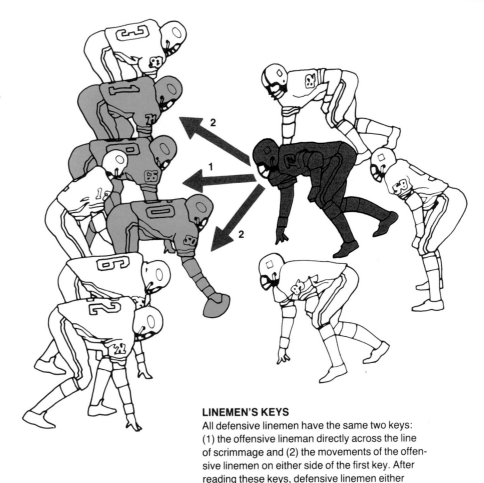

LINEMEN'S KEYS

All defensive linemen have the same two keys: (1) the offensive lineman directly across the line of scrimmage and (2) the movements of the offensive linemen on either side of the first key. After reading these keys, defensive linemen either rush the quarterback or locate the ball carrier.

LINEBACKER, SECONDARY KEYS

The middle linebacker (or the two inside linebackers in a 3-4) keys the center and two guards. He watches their first movements off the line of scrimmage to determine his own action. The strongside linebacker's first key is the tight end. If the tight end stays in and blocks, the linebacker assumes the play is going to be a run; if the tight end releases, it's most likely a pass. The linebacker then checks the running lane (the lane behind, and parallel to, the line of scrimmage) where guards run when pulling on a rushing play. If there is a guard moving

through the lane, the strongside linebacker will step up and take on the block to disrupt the play. If not, he will look for the first running back coming into his area. The weakside linebacker has the same keys as the strongside linebacker except his first read is the running lane because there is no tight end on his side.

Like the strongside linebacker, the strong safety first checks whether the tight end releases off the line or stays in to block. If he releases, the safety plays for the pass; if he blocks, either the safety or the cornerback will come up to force (see page 67)

the play. His second key is the strongside guard or tackle. If either one pulls his way (direction), he comes up to turn, or force, the play inside while the cornerback covers in the secondary.

The free safety keys the uncovered offensive lineman (the player who *hasn't* got a defensive player lining up on him). When the lineman sets up to pass block, the free safety plays for the pass. If he pulls down the line or run blocks, the safety plays for the run.

The cornerback's keys are contingent on what the safeties do.

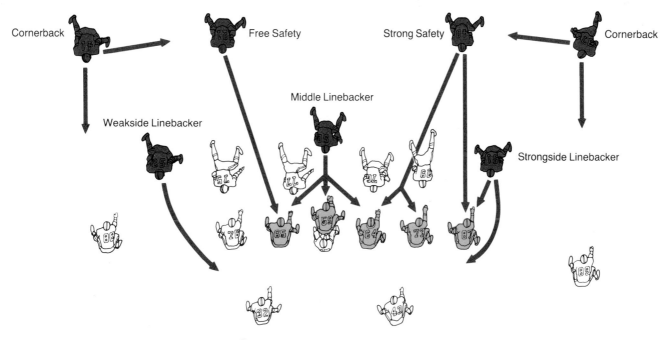

61

Reading the Quarterback

As a pass play develops, zone defenders have a constant key to read—the quarterback. They read his eyes to see which receiver's route he is watching. They read his drop—three, five, or seven steps—to determine how deep a pattern is being run. (Generally, the deeper a quarterback drops, the deeper a pass will be.) And, they read the passer's shoulder action to know when to look for the ball in the air.

Obviously, quarterbacks are aware they are being read and take measures to give out false clues to the action of the play. An experienced quarterback can be particularly adept at not looking at his primary receiver until the last possible second, disguising his drop, and making pump (arm) fakes. It's all part of the cat-and-mouse game between the quarterback and the defense.

The depth of a quarterback's drop can indicate how long a pass he is intending to throw. He takes a three-yard drop for a short, quick pass, a five-yard drop for a medium-range pass, and a seven-yard drop for a long pass (or a delayed pass such as a screen).

Defensive Shifts

In the 1950s and early 1960s, defenses usually lined up in a straight or "even" 4-3. In an even alignment, the defensive linemen play directly across from the offensive linemen. Defenses continued to use the even set up, but offensive teams soon learned how to exploit it. Then came the defensive innovation of the overshift and undershift.

In a true overshift, all four members of the defensive line shift one position over toward the strongside of the offensive formation. An undershift is exactly the opposite; the defensive line shifts *away* from the strongside. There are variations to both these types of shifts, the most basic being that only some of the defensive linemen shift.

Defenses use overshifts and undershifts to gain an advantage at the point where they feel the offensive team is going to attack.

OVERSHIFT

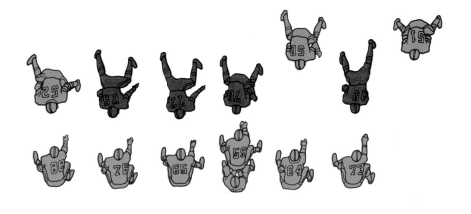

UNDERSHIFT

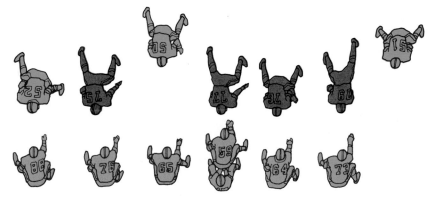

Stacks, Stunts, Slants, and Pinches

Keeping an offense off-balance and confused is a prerequisite for a successful defense.

NFL defenses use a variety of different tactics throughout a game to keep the offense guessing. Very rarely will an offense see the same positioning of all defensive players twice in one game. They are constantly moving around, setting up in different positions, and always experimenting — trying to expose and take advantage of weaknesses found in the offense.

Stacks, stunts, slants, and pinches are some of the most common of these tactics.

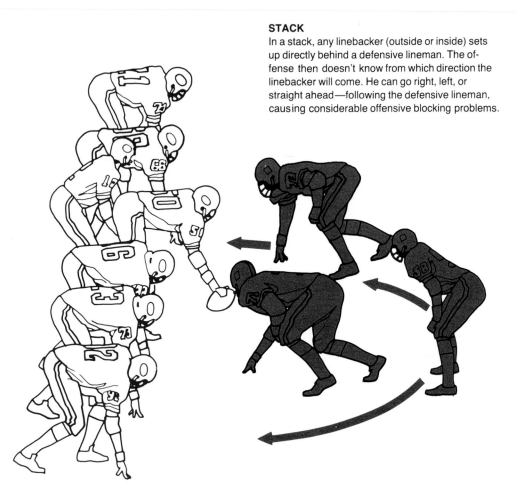

STACK

In a stack, any linebacker (outside or inside) sets up directly behind a defensive lineman. The offense then doesn't know from which direction the linebacker will come. He can go right, left, or straight ahead — following the defensive lineman, causing considerable offensive blocking problems.

SLANTS

A slant is a planned charge by a defensive lineman to the left or right instead of straight ahead. The advantage lies with the defensive lineman, because he knows where he is going from the time he positions himself.

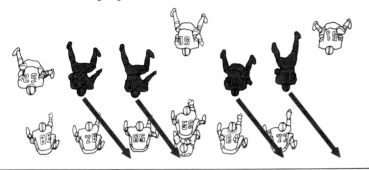

PINCH

In the pinch tactic, the defensive linemen position themselves in the gaps between offensive blockers and "pinch" against one offensive lineman. The charge by the linemen who are pinching render that blocker helpless.

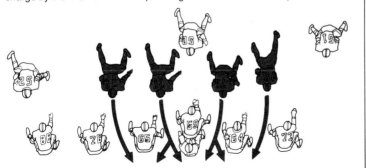

STUNTS

On a stunt, defenders exchange their rushing routes, by looping around each other after the ball has been snapped. Stunts can involve defensive players in any combination—linemen with each other, linemen with linebackers, and so on. The objective of a stunt is to take advantage of, or create, gaps and confusion in the offensive line.

Dogs and Blitzes

The purpose of a pass rush is to increase pressure on an offense, particularly the quarterback. To maximize this pressure, defenses occasionally rush extra men from unexpected positions.

In a dog, a *linebacker* (or any combination of linebackers) leaves his regular area of coverage and streaks past the line of scrimmage, simultaneous with the snap, into the backfield through available holes in the offensive line.

In a blitz, secondary men—alone, together, or in combination with linebackers—try to get to the quarterback. Whereas a dog can be played to stop the run as well as the pass, the blitz is used primarily to stop only the pass (and leaves the defense vulnerable to the run). Cornerbacks blitz from their outside positions and safeties come from their deep areas straight upfield. Safeties must time their blitzes perfectly; they must be careful not to show their blitz or commit too early.

When a defensive player dogs or blitzes, he has the element of surprise in his favor. A player must disguise the fact he is coming, especially from the quarterback. If a quarterback at the line can sense that a dog or blitz is imminent, he can call an audible that could take advantage of the situation. Of course, sometimes defenders tip-off a blitz intentionally—and falsely—to make the quarterback change plays.

DOG: The only real difference between a dog and a blitz is the personnel involved. Dogs are surprise pass rushes by linebackers.

BLITZ: Pass rush maneuvers by safeties and cornerbacks, as well as linebackers working in combination with one or more defensive backs, are blitzes.

Force

There are certain areas of the field that a defense must protect at all costs. One of the most crucial of these is the outside on a running play.

A safety or cornerback (depending on which way an outside play is being run) must not let a ball carrier get outside him, because he could be the last defender between a runner and the goal line. Either player has to force the run back towards the middle of the field (or formation) where his teammates are pursuing the play.

Determining who the force man will be depends on the split of the wide receiver. If a receiver sets up less than 10 yards outside his nearest teammate, the cornerback usually will be the force man; more than 10 yards, and the safety usually has the responsibility.

After the offensive team lines up, the safeties and cornerbacks communicate back and forth. Then the strong safety calls who will force and who will stay back in pass defense.

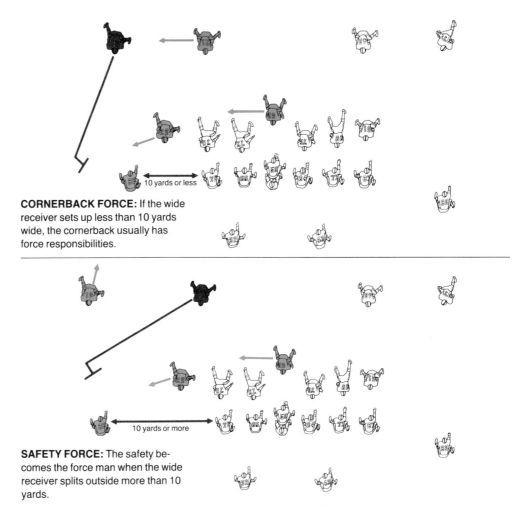

CORNERBACK FORCE: If the wide receiver sets up less than 10 yards wide, the cornerback usually has force responsibilities.

10 yards or less

10 yards or more

SAFETY FORCE: The safety becomes the force man when the wide receiver splits outside more than 10 yards.

Multiple Defensive Backs

As NFL passing attacks continue to become more sophisticated, defenses have to find new ways to cope. One of the most recent defensive ploys has been the use of additional defensive backs.

In a normal 4-3 or 3-4 set, there will be four defensive backs in the game. On some occasions one to three (or more) extra defensive backs are added. When teams go to five defensive backs, they are said to be in a nickel defense; six backs make it a dime. With extra men in the secondary, quarterbacks have a more difficult time finding open receivers. The quarterback never knows which men will be double-teamed or whether any of the defensive backs will blitz.

One of the main justifications for using multiple defensive backs is that offenses are now using up to five receivers on certain plays. Defenses must compensate with additional secondary men; linebackers normally can't cover the additional receivers as well.

The multiple defensive back theory is not without its weaknesses, though. When the linebackers are replaced, the defensive team becomes more vulnerable to the run. An astute quarterback can audiblize to a running play (or run himself) for a big gain instead of forcing a pass into so many defenders.

DOUBLE COVERAGE
When the defense runs extra defensive backs into the game, it is possible to double-team and sometimes even triple-team the offense's most dangerous pass receivers. Who provides the double coverage is important; a defense doesn't want to leave its slower linebackers with single-coverage assignments.

DIME DEFENSE
One response to a pass-oriented attack is to bring in extra defensive backs. Putting in one extra back, making five in all, is known as nickel coverage; two extra backs makes it dime.

Multiple vs. Multiple

NICKEL DEFENSE
The defense uses its extra pass defenders in various combinations. They can play zone alignments and they can play zone on one side of the field and man-to-man on the other. Here, the fifth back covers the running back coming out of the backfield on the weakside.

FIVE ELIGIBLE RECEIVERS
In sure passing situations, the offense tries to stretch the pass defense with as many receivers as possible.

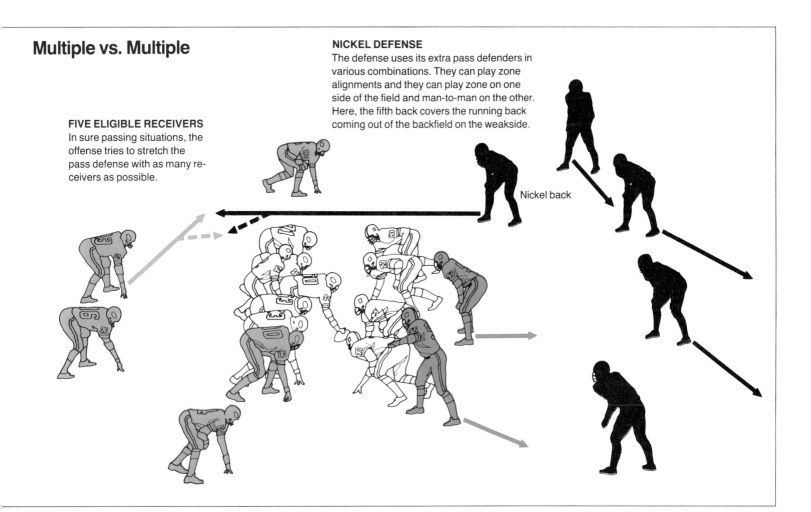

Nickel back

Zones

The basic idea of a zone defense is deceptively simple. Seven or eight defensive players (linebackers and defensive backs), depending on whether the team is playing a 4-3 or 3-4, each run to a prearranged area of the field called a *zone.* They stay in the effective centers of their zones, alert to, but not reacting to where the receivers go, until the ball is thrown. Once the ball is in the air, they converge on the receiver.

In any zone defense, there are two areas that are covered—short zones and deep zones. A defensive player assigned to a short zone is responsible for an area roughly 10 to 20 yards downfield. Someone assigned to a deep zone has a much larger area of responsibility. He covers all the way back to the goal line, if necessary.

The two most basic zone defenses used in the NFL today are illustrated at right.

ROTATING ZONES (STRONG)

The defense divides the passing area into four short zones and three deep zones. In a 4-3 alignment, the three linebackers and one defensive back (usually a cornerback) take the short zones. The two safeties and the other cornerback retreat into the deep zones. Because the linebackers go in one direction and the safeties move the opposite way, the effect is one of "rotation."

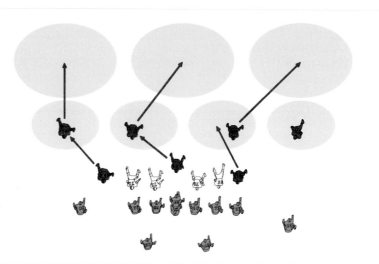

WEAK ZONE

The assignments in the weak zone are the opposite of the strong zone. There still is the same rotation effect, but it goes counterclockwise away from the strongside of the formation. From a 3-4 defense, the rotating zone positions can stay the same (and have a dogging linebacker), or can become a four short, four deep zone set, or five short, two deep.

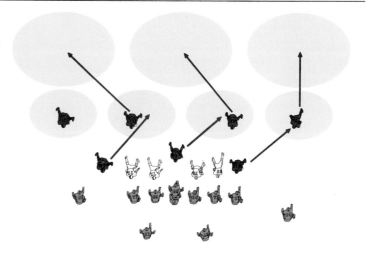

DOUBLE ZONES

In this alignment, the defense divides the field into five short zones and two deep zones. Both corner-backs and all three linebackers (in the 4-3) play the short zones, which still allows for a strong four-man pass rush. (In a 3-4, one linebacker rushes.)

The two safeties cover the deep zones, paying particular attention to the wide receivers, since the double zone is primarily aimed at checking off the wide receivers both short and deep. Defenders must be wary, however, of a fast tight end breaking free into the yawning gap between the two safeties.

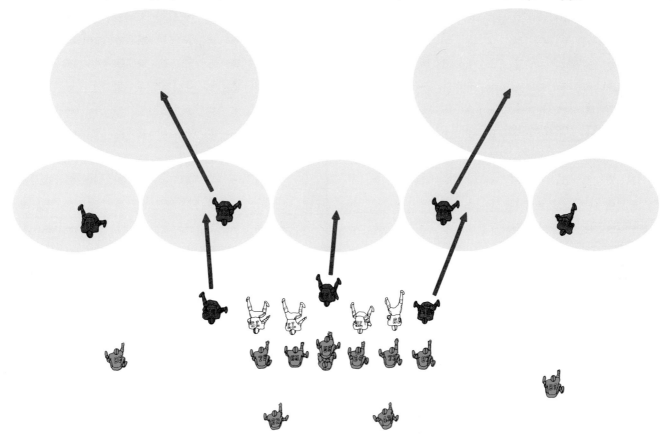

Man-to-Man

The offensive advantage of knowing where the pass play is going is magnified against a man-to-man defense. Quarterbacks try to get the ball to receivers who draw single, man-to-man coverage.

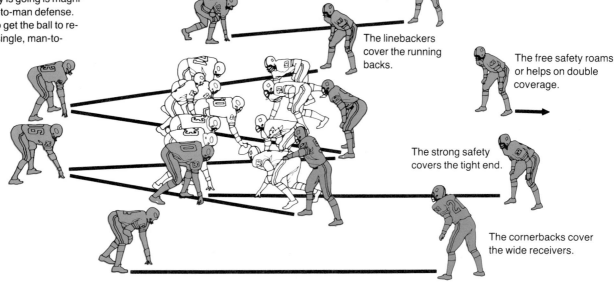

The linebackers cover the running backs.

The free safety roams or helps on double coverage.

The strong safety covers the tight end.

The cornerbacks cover the wide receivers.

The man-to-man pass defense, which was the most common pass coverage in the 1950s and 1960s, has fallen from favor with most coaches in the NFL today because it is very risky and few players learn the necessary techniques in college.

In a straight man-to-man, the linebackers cover the running backs (if they come out of the backfield on a pass pattern); the cornerbacks cover the wide receivers; the strong safety covers the tight end; and the free safety "roams." The free safety also may help double-team an opponent's most dangerous receiver. The cornerbacks have the toughest job in man-to-man coverge. They must keep the receiver between themselves and the quarterback. Backpedaling off the line, a cornerback mirrors every move the receiver makes until the ball is thrown, and then he moves in, timing his hit to the ball's arrival, or cutting in front of the receiver to intercept or bat down the pass.

The major drawback of man-to-man coverage is that it is essentially a personnel match-up, one which sometimes turns into a footrace to the ball. With often only one defender between the goal line and the offense's best wide receiver, one defensive misstep could mean six points. And coaches today, in most cases, aren't willing to put that much responsibility on one player's shoulders.

Bump and Run

The bump and run is a trailing technique used by defensive backs (most often cornerbacks) when they are matched against a wide receiver one-on-one.

In the typical bump and run situation, a defensive back will position himself directly over the receiver. As the receiver comes off the line of scrimmage, the defensive back's first move is to make contact (a bump). The defensive back can only hit the receiver within five yards of the line; beyond that it is considered illegal contact.

After the intitial bump, the defensive back will trail right behind the receiver. The back must never take an inside fake; if he does the receiver can run right past him. He can take an outside fake and let the receiver run to the middle, because that's where his defensive help is.

The defensive back must concentrate totally on the receiver. He cannot worry when the pass is going to be thrown; he does not even look back for the ball until the receiver does. All he is trying to accomplish in the bump and run is to break up the pass play. The only time he should have a chance at an interception is when the ball is poorly thrown.

1. In the bump and run, the defensive back positions himself right over the receiver.

2. As the receiver breaks off the line of scrimmage, the back bumps him.

3. After the initial contact, the back covers the receiver downfield.

4. When the receiver looks back for the ball, the back tries to break up the play.

Special Teams

Kickoffs

On a kickoff, the ball is placed on the kicking team's 35 yard line. Members of the kickoff team are assigned positions to the left or right of the kicker (L1-L5 and R1-R5) based on two criteria: players with considerable pursuit skills line up closest to the ball, fanning out to those with the most speed. Aggressiveness is required in the middle to break through the returner's wedge (see page 77); outside, speed is necessary to run around the wedge. Discipline also is important because kickoff coverage men *must* stay in their lanes until they converge on the ball carrier.

Teams occasionally will position the kicker away from the center of the field towards one of the sidelines (offset him) to reduce the return options of the receiving team.

Squib Kicks

In order to avoid kicking to a dangerous return man, and to foil returns in general, a kicker can squib kick the ball (it also can happen unintentionally). When a squib kick (a low, line drive) hits the field, it usually starts bounding crazily, which makes it more difficult to handle. The effectiveness of the squib kick was never more apparent than in Super Bowl XVI. San Francisco kicker Ray Wersching took advantage of the hard artificial surface in the Pontiac Silverdome to continually blunt the Cincinnati returns with bouncing kicks, which the Bengals' return men had difficulty recovering.

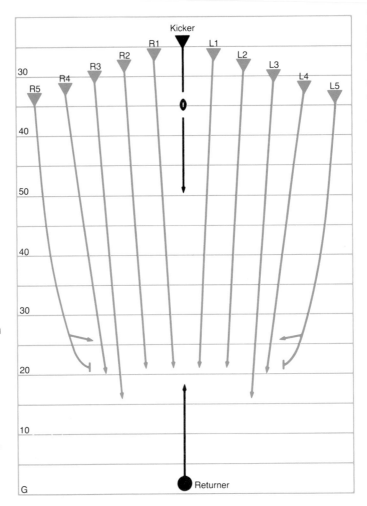

The kickoff team contains two five-man sides plus the kicker. L1 and R1 confront the middle of the return wedge. L2 and R2, L3, and R3 slide inside maintaining leverage on their sides of the field. L4 and R4 have the option to go around the wedge, but must fold back inside if the wedge breaks up the middle. L5 and R5 have the primary containment obligation. Making the tackle is their responsibility if the kick returner reaches the outside. The kicker himself hangs back as a safety valve, sometimes becoming the last hope to stop a returner who has broken free.

Kickoff Returns

There are three separate groups of players on a kickoff return team.

The first wave consists of five blockers, who line up on the opponent's 45 or 50 yard line. Their first assignment is to guard against a possible onside kick (see page 78). Once the ball is kicked off, they retreat to a predetermined spot to block for the kick returner. The five players included in this group are usually quick offensive or defensive linemen, or linebackers who also are excellent blockers.

The second group comprises a four-man wedge of blockers, who position themselves on or about their 20 or 25 yard line. The wedge men have the most critical blocking assignments. They are the ones who clear the path for the return man by knocking down the first wave of tacklers.

The third group consists of the two return men, who set up near the goal line to receive the kickoff. Kick returners usually are either running backs, wide receivers, or defensive backs—players who are used to handling the ball. There are three prerequisites for their assignment: good hands, speed, and courage—they are the prey of at least 10 men barreling down the field at full speed.

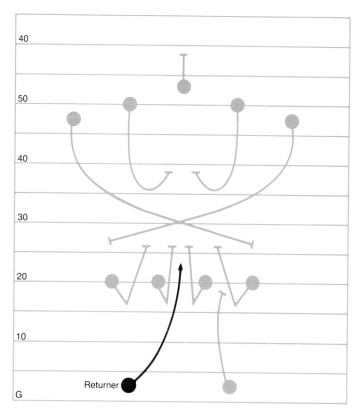

The middle men in the front five drop back 10-15 yards, keying on coverage men L1, R1, and the kicker (see illustration, page 76). The ends carry out a crossing action during their retreat, which puts them in position to block the kicking team's L4 and R4, who have the best angles to make the tackle. Meanwhile, the wedge men watch the flight of the kick, following the ball until it is caught by one of the return men. After retreating to within approximately 10 yards of where the kick is caught, the wedge will suddenly form and move forward to confront the oncoming tacklers. Once one of the two kick returners fields the kick, the other becomes the outside man on his side of the wedge. Kick return plays are called before the kickoff. But a kick returner must remain alert to openings that form away from the predetermined return lanes.

Dick Vermeil on Special Teams:
"If you have enthusiastic special teams, you have good special teams—no matter how they block, tackle, or run."

Walt Michaels on Special Teams:
"Everyone has some fear. A man who has no fear belongs in a mental institution. Or on special teams."

Onside Kicks

A kickoff becomes a free (anybody's) ball once it has traveled at least 10 yards. An onside kick takes advantage of this rule; the kicking team's objective is to recover the ball *before* the receiving team can get to it—instead of conceding possession by kicking it far downfield. Consequently, the players required for executing an onside kick must be quick, in addition to having good hands.

Onside kicks are most frequently used late in a game by a team that is (1) behind, (2) in need of at least one more possession for a scoring opportunity, and (3) racing the clock. They aren't often tried at any other time because if the receiving team *does* recover the ball (as it will most of the time), it will have much better field position—usually near the 50—than on a regular kickoff.

An onside kick can either be kicked softly in a short arc or as a hard line drive—much like a squib kick. The kicker tries to aim the ball at a predetermined area, 10 yards (or just slightly beyond) away so that the kicking team can make a legal recovery.

However, no matter the type of kick, deception is the kicking team's greatest ally; its chances for recovering an onside kick increase dramatically if the receiving team doesn't suspect one is coming. Therefore, a coach may initially send in his regular kickoff team to help disguise the fact that his team is going to attempt an onside kick.

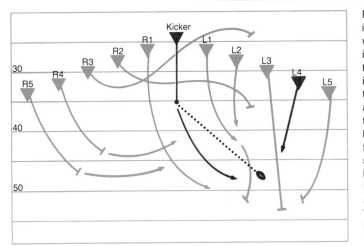

Recovering an onside kickoff is the responsibility of L4 when the ball is kicked left (R4 if it is kicked to the right). L5 tries to contain it, to place L4 in the optimum recovery position. L1, L2, and L3 also may attempt to cover the ball, but they are primarily expected to block in front. R1 crosses the field and becomes the near safety. R3 retreats and becomes the deep safety. R2, R4, and R5 are alert for a return to their side of the field. The kicker goes directly for the ball.

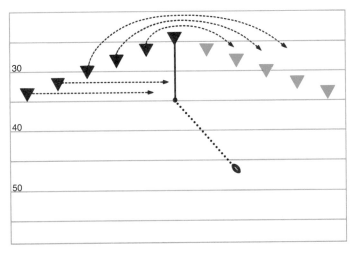

If it's late in the game, and the players on both teams are on the lookout for an onside kick, the kicking team has nothing to hide. The ploy many coaches will use in that situation is a quick shift of players from one side of the field to the other, followed by an onside kick to the overloaded side. It is a desperate attempt by the kicking team, but it can work because of the extra men going after the ball.

Recovering Onside Kicks

When the receiving team suspects an onside kick is coming, especially late in the game, it will insert its own onside specialists into the game. Like the players on the kicking team, they are players with good hands who are accustomed to handling the ball, such as wide receivers, tight ends, running backs, and defensive backs. These men are positioned 10 yards from where the ball is being kicked, usually near the 45 yard line.

If the kickoff team sees an onside recovery alignment in place and decides to scramble the receiving team's strategy by kicking the ball deep instead of delivering the anticipated onside kick, it reduces the opportunity for a lengthy return by the receiving team.

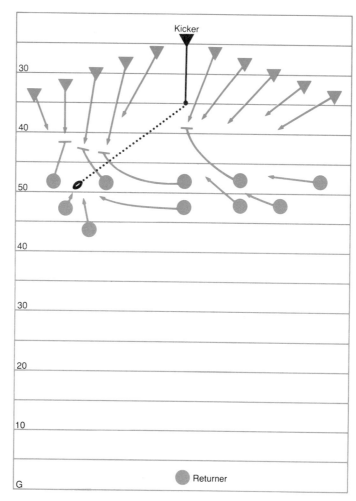

When anticipating an onside kickoff attempt, the return team will substitute special personnel, usually sure-handed receivers, for its normal kickoff return players (i.e., linemen and line-backers). Players in most onside kick situations are instructed to field any kick to their side, but not to advance the ball. Once the ball is fielded, the safest option is to simply fall to the ground—protecting the ball to ensure possession.

Field Goals / Points After Touchdowns

There are two ways a team can score by kicking the ball: points after touchdowns (also called PATs, extra points, or conversions) and field goals.

In both cases the ball must be kicked from a spot on the ground (it is positioned vertically, at a slight angle, by a holder) between the uprights and over the crossbar of the goal post. Extra points are worth one point and only are kicked after a touchdown has been scored. The ball initially is placed on the 3 yard line, then is snapped to the holder and kicked from about the 10 yard line. Since the goal post is set 10 yards deep in the end zone, extra point attempts are approximately 20-yard kicks. Though they are relative "chip shots" for NFL kickers, they are not automatic; the outcomes of countless games have been decided by the margin of an extra point.

Field goals, which are executed in the same basic manner as conversions, are worth three points and can be kicked from any spot on the field, though they are rarely attempted beyond the 40 yard line.

Soccer-style kickers ("sidewinders") have become predominant in the NFL. They approach the ball from an angle, swing their leg sideways, and kick the ball with their instep. The straight-on (conventional) kicker was the only type of kicker in the NFL before the mid-1960s. Conventional kickers approach

On field goal and extra point attempts, a holder kneels approximately seven yards behind the line of scrimmage; the kicker stands two steps behind or beside him (depending on the kicker's style). At the snap, the tight ends (usually there will be two tight ends for placekicks), tackles, guards, and center charge at the defensive players across from them, driving them back. The two men set back from the line are responsible for any outside rush.

There must be perfect coordination between the center, who snaps the ball; the holder, who catches it and places it on the ground; and the kicker. The entire process must be accomplished in a fraction over one second, often in the face of a heavy rush.

the ball facing forward and kick it with their toes (most use a special shoe with a metal cap to protect their toes). Shoes aren't necessarily a prerequisite for kickers; recently there have been several barefoot kickers in the NFL.

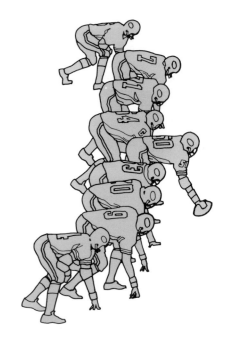

There actually is a third way to score on a kick—the drop kick—which has not been used for years, though it still is a legal way to kick field goals. A drop kick starts off like a punt, but the kicker allows the ball to hit the ground, then kicks it on the bounce.

Blocking Kicks

Field goals and extra points (as well as punts) can be blocked by the defensive team. When that happens, it usually is the result of a mistake by the kicking team. Because of the short time involved in getting a kick off, if there is a good snap, a good hold, and the line blocking is reasonably competent, it is difficult for any defensive man to penetrate before the ball is in the air.

The longer the kick, however, the more chance there is for a block. Most kickers take at least a tenth of a second longer to hit the ball from beyond 40 yards. There also is a lower trajectory, due to the increased distance. As a result, more long field goal attempts are blocked than short ones.

Most members of the field goal/extra point blocking teams are tall defensive linemen and linebackers who are accustomed to pass rushing. These players fill in the middle areas along the line of scrimmage and either try to break through the offensive line to block the kick or leap high in the air to bat down a low kick. The players on the outside of the defensive line (chosen for their quickness) actually are the players with the best chance of blocking an attempt, because of their direct, and sometimes unimpeded angle to the backfield. Two or three players usually are set deep (on long field goal attempts) to guard against gadget plays (see page 84) or to return a kick that falls short of the end zone.

In the kick blocking play below, 3 takes the tight end inside, opening the way for 1 and 2 to block the kick. Number 1 sprints to the outside shoulder of the covering upback. If the upback blocks down on 1, he pulls outside, making room for 2 to rush and try to block the kick. 2 lines up on the outside shoulder of the end. If the upback blocks down on 2, he pulls to make room for 1. Whichever player has the best shot at the ball pursues his rush, aiming for a spot in front of the placement (of the ball) to block the kick.

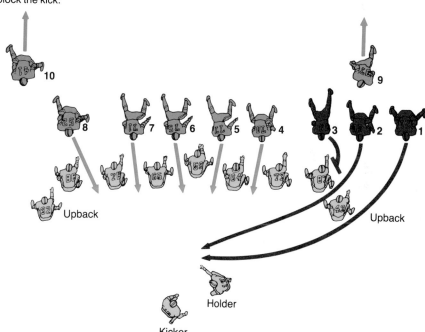
Upback

Upback

Holder

Kicker

Punts/Punt Coverage

In addition to the punter, the punt coverage team is comprised primarily of defensive players, whose collective aim is to stop the return man as quickly as possible after he catches the ball. Linebackers are ideal punt coverage men, since they usually are the surest, best pursuing, and most aggressive tacklers.

The players who man the two outside positions for the punting team are allowed to advance beyond the line of scrimmage before the ball is punted. They must be able to maneuver around blocks by members of the return team and have the speed to get downfield quickly—sometimes before the return man even has a chance to catch the ball. This job usually belongs to cornerbacks and safeties.

The center, as on field goals and extra points, has a crucial assignment on punts. He must snap the ball—very accurately—approximately 15 yards, which is the distance the punter stands back from the line of scrimmage.

The fullback, who stands between the center and punter (at a slight angle, so he won't interfere with the snap), must be a very reliable blocker, able to pick up any rusher who breaks through the line. There also are two other blockers in the backfield, called upbacks, who stand just behind the linemen to either side of the center. These backfield blockers reinforce the middle of the line, which receives the most pressure from the defense.

Usually it is the ends (who can leave before the punt is away) who will contain the return man or down the punt if it is allowed to hit the ground and roll. (The punting team cannot recover its own punt unless it is fumbled or muffed by the receiving team. If a member of the punting team is the first player to touch the ball following a punt, the play is whistled dead and the receiving team assumes possession at that spot.) If the return man signals a fair catch, the defenders are not allowed to touch him (nor can he advance the ball).

Returner

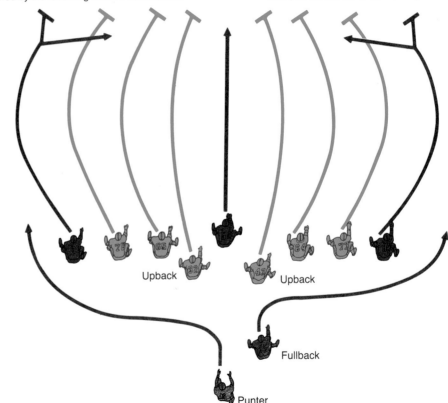

Punt Blocks/Punt Returns

The most common technique in blocking a punt is to overload—massing an unexpected number of players against one part of the offensive line. In an all-out effort to get to the punter and block the punt, all 10 members of the punt block team (excluding only the punt returner) can be assigned to rush.

The offensive center is a prime candidate to be attacked by a punt-blocking team, simply because he has the difficult assignment of making the long snap to the punter and will be off balance for a split second afterward.

Punt Returns

When a team decides to return a punt (instead of trying to block it), every member on the return team knows which way it will be run back (left, right, or middle) before the punt occurs. Punt returners rarely freelance or bring the ball back in any direction they please, though it often looks as if they do.

Returning punts is one of the most dangerous jobs on the field. When a punt is in the air, the returner must concentrate totally on the flight of the ball. He then has several choices: He can catch the ball and run with it through a swarming maze of tacklers; he can wave his arm in the air (while the punt is in flight) and call for a fair catch; or, if the punt appears too difficult to handle, he can let it bounce and roll dead.

One advantage for the return man is that he

The punt block illustrated here is a concerted rush with seven men coming from different angles to reach the punter. The two outside players (1 and 9) hold up (block) their men and then follow them downfield, trying to keep them away from the return man (if the punter is successful in getting off his punt).

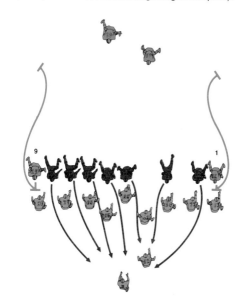

can't be hit until he touches the ball. But once he touches it (unless he has called for a fair catch), he is fair game. The returner must have enough quickness and guile to quickly elude the first wave of tacklers, or the play will end before it can get started.

In the diagram below of a punt return, the ends (1 and 9) take the players directly across from them out of the play. Each remaining lineman picks up a man, trying to deny access to the return lane. Number 8 tries to block the punt. The deep back fields the punt. The upback, just in front of the returner, blocks.

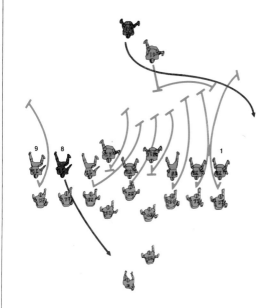

Mike Ditka on Punt Returns:
"Inside the ten, you field nothing, and here's why: Most kicks bouncing inside the ten will find their way into the end zone."

Special Teams Gadget Plays

Teams can resort to trick or gadget plays when lining up in a special teams formation, just as they can from running or passing formations.

Onside kicks are an example of a special teams play that can involve the element of surprise. Another example is a reverse on a kick-off return, where the back who initially receives the ball hands it off to a teammate who is running in the opposite direction. There are a number of other special teams gadget plays, especially those associated with punts and field goals. These gadgets can be either runs or passes. On pass plays, the holder or punter throws a pass to an end who has released instead of blocking. Here are two basic examples of special teams gadgets.

FAKING A FIELD GOAL

Most holders on field goals are quarterbacks, because of their ball handling abilites (they are used to taking snaps and can place the ball easily on kicks). Their expertise in running offensive plays also comes in handy.

The holder's first assignment, before he calls the snap signals, is to examine the defense to determine if there is an overload to one side of the line (which may signify an all-out block attempt).

For example, if the holder sees a defensive overload to the right side of the line (six men to the right of the center), he may call an audible for a gadget play, because he knows the defense will be vulnerable on the side away from the overload. In that case, instead of placing the ball for a kick when he receives the snap, the holder will stand up and roll out to the left side of the line with three options: (1) he can continue to run the ball himself; (2) he can pass to the left upback, who, after hearing the audible, will release downfield as a receiver; or (3) he can pitch the ball back to the kicker, who has trailed the holder down the line on a parallel course, anticipating a lateral.

If this play is executed properly, it is almost impossible for an overloaded defense to stop.

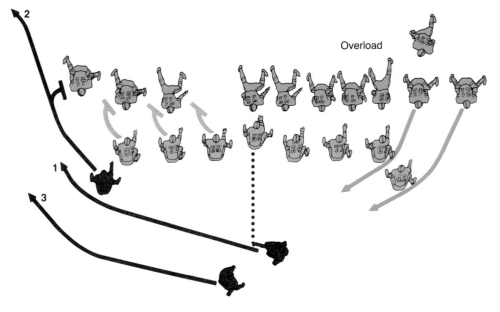

FAKING A PUNT

The most common *planned* gadget play from punt formation calls for the fullback (or the player who lines up between the center and punter) to receive the snap directly from the center (illustrated here). After catching the snap, the fullback then runs to a designated hole. He often has blocking help from one or both of the upbacks, who lead him through the hole or to the outside. This gadget is used when the punting team only has a few yards (rarely more than five) to go for a first down.

The most common *unplanned* gadget play from punt formation involves the spontaneous actions of the punter. If he sees an opening in the defense and feels he can pick up the necessary yardage for his team to maintain possession, the punter may try to run the ball. This move is often unknown to any other person on the field (or even the coach on the sideline). It can be very successful if the punter catches the defense napping; it can turn into a costly gaffe if it fails.

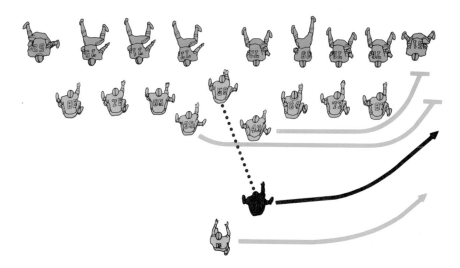

Game Plan
Behind the Scenes
Rules
Glossary and Index

Gillman on the Game Plan:

"The first thing you have to know about all game plans is this: They are really not that complicated, and they usually are overrated.

"Basically there is no magic about a game plan. There is no way you can sit behind a projector for 185 hours or something, and, presto, come up with an idea that's going to make people disappear.

"You just do your homework, take your basic stuff, and adapt it to what you think will be the best way to deal with what the opposition is doing.

"The big thing is to give it a different look. You may use different sets. You may use motion. But you won't add that many things. There just isn't time.

"You're not just looking to see where you want to throw the ball or run the ball. What you're looking for is reaction and over-reaction on the part of the defense.

"The reason for that is, I want the big play. I don't want the little play, the average play. I want the big play. . . .

"Your game plan is well started out Monday night. You hope by Tuesday night you have it pretty well formulated. Wednesday, it should be done. But, dang it, sometimes it's not done until Friday.

"You're making changes, adding, subtracting, changing formations. But you don't dare change your basic offense, like a lot of people think a coach does. Coaches who do that sort of thing lose.

"You build your offense from your basic running game, from what I like to call our 'Dirty Dozen.' It's as good a name as any for twelve plays we think are the best twelve plays our talent will let us run. We're going to maintain and keep polishing all these basic things because we know them well, and we're going to work like hell on execution.

"Now we expand our selection to the 'Dirty Dozen Plus Four.' What's Plus Four? It's any special plays we think can be designed to beat the people we're playing.

"That's the maximum number you might add. It might be only Plus One or Plus Two. The more changes you make, the worse execution you're going to get. The result is you wind up getting beat.

"Once we've established what we're hoping to do on the ground, the next decision is what formations do we want to run. We're going to run the Dirty Dozen Plus Four, but we're going to give you a different look.

"How much motion shall we put to those plays? What kind of motion?

"Essentially, no matter who you're playing, you have a basic passing game just like your basic running game. You have so many passes to the tight end, so many passes to the strongside end, so many to the weakside end and running backs. It's all patterned.

"Again, we are going to decide, based on film study, what formations we want to run this out of. Do we want to use movement?

"Again, what you're looking for is over-reaction. Frequently, that will happen on a pass off play action. Play action passes are the keys to the big play off the passing game. And big plays win football games.

"Now we add what I call 'deceptions.' These would be the screens, at least three types, and the draws. They are the plays that keep people honest against your passing game, that prevent them from just teeing off on you.

"After the deceptions come the gadget plays—the reverses and bootlegs and things like that. You might run them only once a game, or maybe not at all. But you need the threat of them. The defense needs to know they are there.

"These are the basic elements of a game plan, omitting, of course, the kickoff, punt, and placement special teams, and the deceptions [onside kick, fake kick, etc.] that must go with them.

"Naturally, there also is the flip side—the defensive game plan that must be developed to counter all those schemes being developed by all the coaches on the other team."

In the Booth

During an NFL game, every team's coaching staff is divided into two units. One unit, including the head coach, is stationed on one sideline of the field with the players. The other unit mans a booth in the press box. They are in constant communication with each other via telephone headsets.

As pro football strategy has grown more complex, so has the reliance on input from the assistant coaches in the press box, who are responsible for providing the field coaches with play-by-play updates on what they see happening on the field.

The game is entirely different from the press box. While the coaches on the field inevitably get caught up in the heat of the action, the coaches in the press box can view the game almost as they would view a scouting film. They can watch offensive and defensive strategy develop, and identify trends.

Naturally, there is some emotion in the coaches' press box booth, but the atmosphere isn't as frantic as it is on the sidelines. The press box coaches are allowed to concentrate more on Xs and Os and discern just what is happening down on the field. They watch the 22 men moving about as though they were on a vast green chess board.

The coaches in the press box are responsible for picking up the little things that can turn a game around. They'll notice when a linebacker is cheating toward the sideline if he

has guessed that a running play has been called. They'll watch to see if an opponent is taking the proper lanes of pursuit on defense. They'll check carefully to watch how the opponent reacts to new formations. And they'll observe — and report — any subtle flaws in their own team's play that might not be picked up by the coaches at field level.

One of the tools of the press box coaches is a Polaroid camera. The coaches photograph the game from the upstairs booth, and the pictures show in freeze frame the formation schemes (both offensive and defensive) at the snap of the ball. The photos are studied by the other coaches and players in

the locker room at halftime.

Since all teams put in at least a few new wrinkles before every game — new plays and formations designed to catch the opponent off guard — it is the responsibility of the press box coaches to quickly identify any new looks and plays, and help make adjustments.

The impact that the press box coaches have on the outcome of a game is reflected in the NFL rule that states that if the communication system in one coaches' booth breaks down, the coaches in the opponent's booth are not permitted to communicate to their sideline, either, until the broken phone lines have been restored.

Adapting to Rule Changes

The success of an NFL team depends in part on its ability to adapt to rule changes instituted by the league. In other words, success is a matter of survival of the most prepared.

Sometimes an apparently subtle rule change can have far reaching effects on pro football strategy. In 1972, the NFL rulemakers moved the hashmarks (the lines that determine placement of the ball before each play from scrimmage) 10 feet 9 inches closer to the center of the field. That put the hashmarks 70 feet 9 inches in from each sideline directly in line with the goalpost uprights, and meant that every play would begin closer to the center of the field.

At the time, it seemed like an innocuous adjustment, a minor alteration of groundskeeping. In fact, it was anything but that. Moving the hashmarks has had a profound effect on the way the game is played.

In the former demarcation, there was always a wide side and short side for every play. Defenses usually were forced to commit their players early (before the snap) in response to the two angles, which gave the quarterback more time to read the defense and call audibles to exploit any weakness he noticed.

But the symmetrical field changed all that. Defensing a balanced field meant a balanced defensive formation. Players did not need to shift into a coverage until the ball was snapped. That helped kill the early "read" and the adventuresome passing that went with it.

Another outgrowth of the symmetrical field was the 3-4 defense. The 3-4 is the ultimate in a balanced formation, with a nose tackle playing over center, a linebacker over either guard, and a tackle over either end. The three-man line also frees as many as eight men for pass defense, making the secondary a very crowded area in which to direct a forward pass.

As a result, NFL passing attacks soon were put on an endangered list. So several years later, some new rules were put into effect, aimed both at closing some of the loopholes caused by the hashmarks changes and opening up the passing game again.

In 1977, defensive backs were restricted to one "chuck" per receiver either in the three-yard zone at or beyond the line of scrimmage or once beyond that zone, instead of the previous unlimited contact until the ball was in the air. Pass blockers were given a little greater freedom of arm movement. And the penalty for offensive holding was reduced from 15 yards to 10.

Those rules provided some relief to passing attacks. But then, in 1978, the pass blocking rules were liberalized still further, to allow a blocker to fully extend his arms with open hands. Also, the rule on contact with receivers was amended to state that continuous contact with a receiver was legal only within the first five yards of the line of scrimmage.

Suddenly, the momentum swung full circle back to the offense. With dammed up pass rushers and secondaries forced to play more "softly," offenses began to pass with abandon again.

This, of course, has forced corresponding adjustments by the defenses. Tighter, more cerebral pass coverages have evolved, including the expanded deployment of specialty substitutions (see page 94). Defenses are stunting and blitzing more than ever, in an attempt to increase the pressure on the quarterback, and defensive backs are being assigned to receivers all through their patterns.

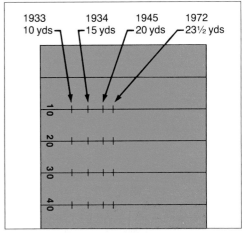

Moving NFL hashmarks just three-and-a-half yards further in profoundly affected game strategy.

Exploiting Tendencies

Every team has its own distinct personality; there are passing teams and running teams, blitzing teams and reading teams, conservative teams and gambling teams. Within these general personality designations, teams ex-

> **Gillman on Tendencies:**
>
> *"I have this big card I always use. I get it from a computer. But we used to do it manually.*
>
> *"On this card, it tells me what you [the opposing team] do on first and ten. It tells me what you do on first and ten of a new series.*
>
> *"I have to know your [defensive] fronts. I have to know your pass coverages. I have to know how many dogs you have and what the nature of your dogs are. What percentage of dogs do you use?*
>
> *"Then, we go to second down. We have second down broken down into second and one-to-three, second and six-minus, second and seven-to-ten, and second and eleven-plus.*
>
> *"Now I have to know all the fronts, coverages and percentage of dogs for these situations. The same thing is true for third down, of course.*
>
> *"As the games goes on, you rely less on what's on the card."*

This computer printout analyzes offensive tendencies in second down and 7-10 yards to go situations.

hibit specific traits, called tendencies, in given situations. Tendencies used to be charted painstakingly by hand from detailed game film analyses. Now, figuring tendencies is done almost exclusively by computer.

Coaches study the tendencies of an upcoming opponent in exhaustive detail to try to uncover any weaknesses or patterns that can be exploited. For instance, if team X's tendency on first down is to run 90 percent of the time, team Y scouting them can set its defenses accordingly—and with confidence—on most first-down situations.

Or, using another example, if team X usually responds to a running situation with a 3-4

defense, team Y, knowing this, either can plan specific running plays to take advantage of the 3-4, or can influence team X into a 3-4 defense simply by using a running formation.

The danger of relying heavily on tendencies is that they are not infallible. All teams scout themselves to determine their own tendencies and become aware of doing things that other teams may be using against them. In the previous example, team X purposely could begin using a 4-3 defense against team Y's run formations to undermine part of team Y's game plan.

Teams are careful, however, of taking such self-analysis so far that they get away from playing in their own distinctive styles.

Adjusting to Situations

Pro football is game of adjustments. The strategy devised in the quiet of a coach's office early in the week can sometimes begin unraveling at the opening kickoff on game day. Consequently, there is no such thing as a concrete game plan; you adjust to what the defense gives and the prevailing situation at the time.

Before the Game

The most obvious factor to which a team must adjust is the weather. Wind, rain (at game time or earlier in the week), snow, and extremes of heat and cold must be considered before a team takes the field; all figure prominently into game strategy. Poor field conditions may require a change of footwear, and, like rain, may necessitate a shift in the balance of the game plan toward the running game. Strong winds also may severely affect the passing game, limiting it to short strikes, and may neutralize even the best field goal kicker. High heat and humidity or below-zero temperatures present problems, the solutions to which may go back to training camp conditioning or involve specially adapted clothing or sideline equipment (e.g. mesh jerseys, long underwear, sideline fans, and heated benches). In the 1981 NFL playoffs, the San Diego Chargers may have faced the ultimate test of preparedness for the elements. Against Miami in the divisional playoff game, the Chargers had to contend with high humidity and temperatures hovering near the 80s. The next week in the conference championship game at Cincinnati, the game-time temperature was 11 below zero, with a wind-chill factor of 59 below zero!

During the Game

As a game progresses, coaches sometimes modify their decisions about what plays will work against their opponent. They arrive at these decisions by feeling out the other team in the early stages of the game. The coaches in the booth also give the head coach and his offensive and defensive coordinators valuable inputs regarding the action on the field. So do the players in the game, particularly the quarterback and defensive captain, who have communicated with the members of their units.

Actually, throughout the game the strategy refinement process goes on. While the offense is on the field, the defense may be on the sideline huddled around a defensive coach, who, chalkboard in hand, is revising certain formations and coverages. During called or officials' time outs, the quarterback makes a beeline for the sideline, where he has quick strategy conferences with the head coach. When the defense is in the game, the quarterback also will confer, via headset, with the coaches upstairs for any additional insights they may be able to add from their high vantage point. They may have spotted, say, a situation where their fastest wide receiver draws only single coverage—a situation perhaps reported earlier to the quarterback in the huddle by the wide receiver himself. The coaches and quarterback file this information away until the proper time to spring it again on the defense.

Of course, not all adjustments are implemented on the sideline. They are constantly taking place on the field as well, creating other matchups besides the ones reflected by the starting lineups.

Halftime

Halftime in a locker room might appear as sheer chaos to an outside observer—but it is organized chaos. The first few minutes after a team leaves the field are devoted to equipment changes, first aid and injury treatment, and just resting. Then the players settle into groups for brief seminars with their position coaches. They close ranks in separate skull sessions, linebackers with linebackers, receivers with receivers, and so on. The head coach paces from group to group, finally settling in with his quarterbacks.

> **Gillman on Halftime:**
> *"At halftime, you just try to pick out the things you have done that have been successful and you decide what you haven't done that might be successful."*

Shortly, the groups coalesce into two meetings—the offense and the defense—each with their respective coordinators. While the defensive coordinator, for instance, admonishes his linemen about being caught in inside traps, the offensive coordinator is explaining a list of plays he thinks will work. These plays were chosen minutes earlier after studying the first-half Polaroid pictures of the opposing defense taken by the coaches in the booth.

Just before taking the field for the second half, the team surrounds the head coach. He addresses the players briefly and matter-of-factly; motivation at this point is an individual responsibility.

Personnel Adjustments

Every so often a starting player has a bad day and must be replaced. Or sometimes a timely substitution can create a glaring mismatch on the field. But, overall, injury is the primary reason for personnel adjustments.

If injuries are known about before a game, adjustments can be made during the practice week. Some injury adjustments, however, are not made until just prior to game time, when it is determined if an injured or recuperating player will see action or not. Adjustments also are made for injuries to opposing players. An opponent, for example, may play an entirely different game without its star running back.

Often the most crippling injury a team can suffer is one that puts the starting quarterback on the bench. Whether the quarterback is going to miss the second half of a game, a number of games, or the whole season, adjustments (including the most extreme— trading for a new quarterback) must be made, according to the experience of his backups. In the unlikely, but still not impossible, event that the starter and all his backups are injured at the same time, most teams have a "disaster quarterback." This player may have been a quarterback in college who was turned into a defensive back or running back in the pros. He is familiar with running the offense and plays quarterback occasionally in practice.

Overtime

When a game is tied at the end of regulation play, an overtime period results. During the regular season, only one extra period is played and the extended game may end in a tie. During postseason play, as many 15-minute overtimes as needed are added until one team wins. The extra period (or periods) also is called "sudden death" or "sudden victory" overtime because the first score of any kind wins the game.

A sudden death period becomes in many ways a separate game in itself, with strategy and tactics revised accordingly. It also is much like a game of pool; you try to set yourself up to score, but if you fail you don't want to leave your opponent with an easy shot.

Most teams will take some chances in an overtime, always weighing the efficacy of each play against the factors of ball control and possession. Obviously, high percentage plays are favored.

For an offense in overtime, field position becomes even more critical than usual, as does the range and accuracy of its field goal kicker. (Like artillery duels, overtimes often are simply exercises in getting kickers into scoring position.) For the defense in overtime, *everything* becomes critical. Any yardage it gives up puts the other team that much closer to ending the game.

Situational Substitution

Every football game is the sum total of its individual plays. Each play, or situation, is unique because of the following four factors: down, distance, score, and time remaining.

It used to be that 11 starters (on offense and defense) played every down from scrim-

mage except when they were injured. Now every team has a different alignment manned by different people to meet every situation.

In a sense, all NFL teams have done is borrow a page from industry. They have discovered that efficiency can be increased if specialists are on the job. So the game is no longer simply one team's best athletes against another team's best athletes for 60 minutes. Instead, it has become "best against best" for each individual situation.

Situational (or specialty) substitution— the practice of inserting specialists into a game based primarily on down and distance—isn't an entirely new concept. There have always been specialists, such as kickers, holders, and long snappers, etc. In some ways, situational substitution is merely an extension of some of the personnel decisions that always have been used for special teams. But the overall concept has become a dominant theme in the formulation of strategy in the NFL.

The constant flow of player substitutions throughout the course of a game has blurred the distinction between starter and reserve. A player who doesn't start a game may often wind up playing more downs than the starter at his position. (In 1981, San Francisco 49ers defensive end Fred Dean, a pass rushing specialist, was named as the NFC's defensive player of the year—even though he rarely started.)

Strategies have become so intricate that

just about any player combination is liable to appear. There are kick blocking specialists, pass rushing specialists such as Dean, and pass protection specialists. At any time you might see three or four wide receivers in the game at once; multiple tight end formations; wing formations (double or triple) that mix various combinations of running backs, wide receivers, and tight ends; a four-man front brought in by a 3-4 team to increase the pressure on the quarterback; an eight-man secondary installed for optimum pass coverage; and so on.

The heavy flow of traffic to and from the sidelines on every play sometimes creates a certain amount of confusion, increasing the chance of having too many—or too few—men on the field when the play begins. (Having too few men on the field is not a penalty; too many men on the field is.)

Coaches play waiting games on the sidelines to gain the upper hand, stalling before sending in their specialty players (in hopes of learning the opponent's strategy by identifying its on-field personnel first).

One way an offense can control the extent of defensive substitutions is to run several plays consecutively without a huddle, a hectic maneuver that precludes the defense from shuttling specialty players into the game because of the abbreviated time between plays.

Situational substitution has had a side benefit for offenses and defenses alike: It has made it easier for more rookies to come into the league and contribute right away. By narrowing the roles of the 45 men on a roster to a point where they can be learned quickly, rookies can be turned into specialists for strictly running or passing downs—so they don't have to immediately learn *all* of the variables and options for every situation they might face.

Situational substitution never ensures success by itself; it merely places a team in its most upright competitive posture. For, in general, a play slumps or stands on execution, not formations.

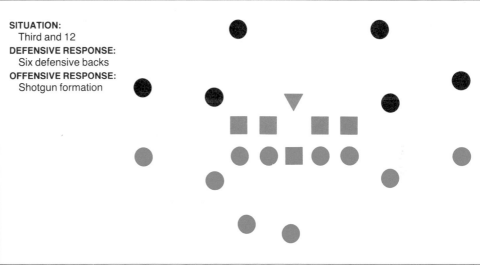

SITUATION:
Third and 12
DEFENSIVE RESPONSE:
Six defensive backs
OFFENSIVE RESPONSE:
Shotgun formation

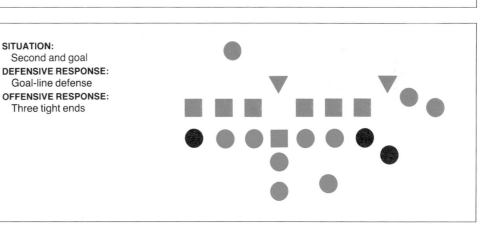

SITUATION:
Second and goal
DEFENSIVE RESPONSE:
Goal-line defense
OFFENSIVE RESPONSE:
Three tight ends

Field Position

One of the factors most strongly weighed in offensive strategy is field position. Where a team is on the field can have as much influence on the next play called as down and distance, the score, and game time remaining. Though no team is completely predictable, field position is an accurate indicator of what an offense or defense may or may not do.

OFFENSIVE DIRECTION ⟶

1

This is the danger zone. One offensive mistake here could mean giving up points. Consequently, the offense generally runs safe, high-percentage plays here. Quarterbacks throw short and to the outside. When pressured, they throw the ball away rather than take a loss. On runs, direct handoffs are preferable; the ball has to be protected at all costs. If possible, a team should get out of this area before punting. And, obviously, turnovers and penalties should be avoided.

2

In this area, the offense can be more wide-open, although a turnover can still give the opposing team an easy scoring opportunity. Teams will gamble here on a long-gainer on first and second down, or will run sweeps and traps. But on third down they usually won't get fancy, concentrating instead on making the first down. When passing on third down, the quarterback should throw for the yardage needed. On fourth down, punters go for distance with their kicks.

3

Almost anything can happen in this area of the field, as teams try to advance into scoring territory. Heavy use of play action passes can be expected. Late in a close game, the defense often gives up short passes and gains here, concentrating more on protecting the deep zones. Punters go for accuracy as well as distance, trying to pin the opposing team deep in its own territory.

4

Inside the 40, punts generally are out of the question. Look for certain field goal attempts by any team that has gotten this far. Late in a game, if a team is behind by more than a field goal, it probably will go for first down yardage or a touchdown on fourth down.

5

This is the scoring zone. To win consistently, a team must get into the end zone from here every time. Inside the 10, strategy and personnel can change. Play selection becomes critical; a play that loses yardage—or a penalty call—can move a team out of scoring range, and a turnover can mean lost points. Play action bootlegs and keepers are run often by quarterbacks, who expect to see more dogs and blitzes. For the team behind by more than a touchdown late in the game, this is "four down territory"; it has no choice but to "go for it."

G   10   20   30   40   50   40   30   20   10   G

First Down

First down may be the most important down of a series. Gains of five yards or more on first down take the pressure off the offense, because on second and short almost anything can work—inside runs, outside runs, traps, misdirections, long or short passes. But small gains, no gains, or losses on first down intensify offensive pressure. The play alternatives quickly narrow down to passes and the defense knows it. That's what the war on first down is all about. The offense fights to stay free of second and long, while the defense pushes to generate those very situations.

On first down, the offense can use its advantage—knowing the play—to the fullest. That's why running on every first down, as most teams used to do and some teams still do, is questionable. It gives the defense what it has not earned: the ability to anticipate.

The defense strives toward the goal of elimination. Because it does not know the play, it seeks to limit the possibilities. It wants to eliminate from consideration what will not occur, so it can play hard against what might. However, as long as the offense varies its attack, the defense cannot eliminate too much. So, to maintain maximum pressure on the defense on first down, the offense must threaten with a balanced mixture of runs and passes.

The standard defenses are combination defenses; what they do best is protect simultan-

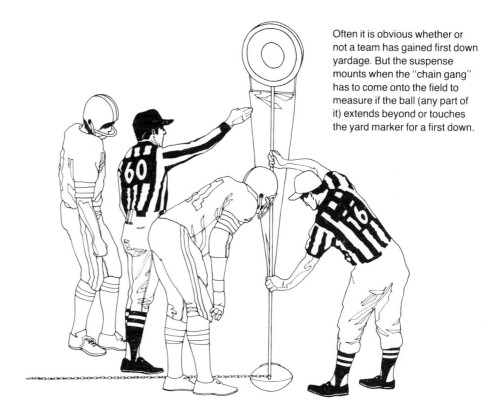

Often it is obvious whether or not a team has gained first down yardage. But the suspense mounts when the "chain gang" has to come onto the field to measure if the ball (any part of it) extends beyond or touches the yard marker for a first down.

eously against the run and the pass. When an offense consistently beats a defense on first down, it remains a threat to run or pass on second or third down as well. Consequently, the defense rarely can move from its standard to its specialty alignments. Further, most teams have pass rush and pass defense specialists who come into the game on obvious passing downs. These players can be tremendous defensive weapons. But if an offense is successful in making substantial gains and mixing its plays on first down, specialty defensive players and units can be neutralized; they can't do much damage if they're not in the game.

The 3-4 in Action

There are reasons why the 3-4 has become the most popular defense in the NFL—and reasons why it took so long to gain wide acceptance.

The 3-4 is a linebacker-oriented defense. Because the three down linemen it employs can be double-teamed by the six offensive linemen (center, guards, tackles, and the tight end) they face, they cannot be expected to generate a heavy pass rush. Instead, the linemen are asked to bulldoze, to hold ground and tie up the blocking, leaving the quarterback sacks to dogging linebackers. When not rushing, the other linebackers backpedal to share coverage in the secondary. Using all four linebackers provides an eight-man sec-

---

Bum Phillips on the 3-4:

"The beauty of the three-four defense is those four linebackers. They give mobile pursuit, cover the field from side to side, and can stop anything in between.

"The three-four also makes it easier to build a quality line. You can get by with a mediocre nose tackle because he lines up across from the center, who has to worry about blocking him and snapping the ball. So all you really need are two good ends, and you can find two outstanding linemen a heck of a lot faster than you can find four."

In order to better camouflage—and maximize—its pursuit of the quarterback, the defense often varies the positioning of its top pass rusher(s) from play-to-play.

ondary, allowing double coverage on most or all receivers in complex zones, more than compensating for the weakened pass rush. On runs, the linebackers react as a unit, swarming toward the hole or pursuing the ball carrier rather than freelancing, as do many of their counterparts in the 4-3.

Some teams recently have devised ways of using the 3-4 that strengthen it further. Employing these new wrinkles, however, is based strictly on the personnel a team has available.

On a running down, for example, a team's best run defender will line up at left end. On a passing down, he may be moved to right end, while the right end shifts to nose tackle, and the team's best *pass* rusher is brought into the game to play left end. It may sound confusing, but such constant shuffling of personnel drives offensive coaches crazy.

A variation of this is to take the best pass rusher and put him where he has the best chance of beating a blocker on a given play—on the line or at linebacker, on the right side or the left. The offense never knows from down to down where he'll line up.

The rise in popularity of the 3-4, and the focus of the formation on linebackers, has had an interesting effect on NFL scouting and drafting. By its nature the 3-4 defense places a premium more on linebacker speed, mobility, and pass-coverage ability than on size. Consequently, NFL linebackers have been getting smaller, faster, and more compact. (They still hit just as hard, though.) Also, colleges produce linebackers in abundance by utilizing four-linebacker sets. And there seems always to be a supply of able but undersized college linemen who can be recast as pro linebackers.

The 4-3 in Action

No one defensive front can do it all, which is why no NFL team uses a 3-4 or 4-3 exclusively; defenses shift according to situations. Many 3-4 teams, for instance, shift to the 4-3 alignment in sure passing situations. They prefer to pressure the quarterback with a strong rush, instead of concentrating on flooding the secondary with additional pass defenders.

However, it is possible to both augment the pass rush *and* get more defenders into the passing zones. This is done by retaining the four-man front and replacing a linebacker with a fifth defensive back—the nickel defense—a tactic that has gained popularity as passing offenses proliferate.

> **Faulkner on the 4-3:**
> *"The key player in the four-three is the middle linebacker. The linemen, in effect, protect him, keeping the blockers away so he can make the tackle."*

Some 4-3 teams choose to strengthen the rush further on certain passing situations by shifting into a five-man front. By doing so they are gambling that the intensified pass rush can get to the quarterback, or disrupt the play, before the quarterback can get the pass off into the unreinforced secondary. There is a good chance the five-man rush will work because offensive lines confront three- and four-

man lines most often; the presence of a fifth defensive lineman can scramble the entire blocking scheme. Teams set in a basic 4-3 also can achieve the same results the five-man line affords, plus gain an added element of surprise, by stunting or dogging one of the three linebackers.

The pressure on the linebackers in the 4-3 is very intense, especially on the man in the middle, who literally is in the middle of everything. Even a moment's hesitation and the play can be on top of him.

Ultimately, however, it is extremely important for the line in the 4-3 to extablish a heavy pass rush on its own terms. If linebackers are called upon to aid the pass rush by dogging too often, the offense can adjust by exploiting the vacant coverage areas created by the charge of the linebacker(s).

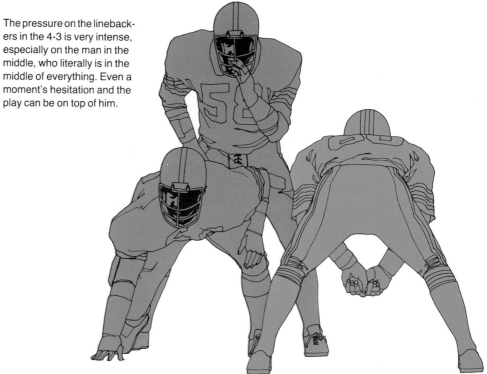

Beating Zones

Passing against a zone defense can be treacherous, but zones no longer exhibit a chokehold on the passing game, which generally was the case throughout the 1970s.

In counterpoint to the considerable variety of zones, which are designed in part to deceive quarterbacks and confuse their "read" of the coverage, there has been a dramatic evolution and refinement of offensive strategies to combat zone coverage.

Since the football field is 100 yards long and 53⅓ yards wide, it is paramount for the offense to use as much of the available field as it can. It does this by stretching the zone, both vertically and horizontally in order to create a larger amount of area for the pass defenders to cover.

That requires a quarterback with a quick release and a strong arm, one who can throw both long (for the vertical stretch) and from sideline-to-sideline (to stretch the zone horizontally). It is also important to have a squadron of fast receivers who can disperse into the secondary and scatter the coverage.

Double and triple wings are among the formations that can help take the intiative away from a zone defense (forcing it out of its original alignment), because additional backs are placed on the periphery of the formation, loading one side with extra pass receivers.

If a quarterback finds the deep defensive backs cheating too much toward one side of

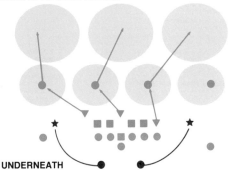

UNDERNEATH

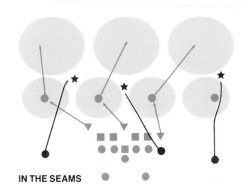

IN THE SEAMS

the ball in response to an overloaded formation, he sometimes can beat the zone by calling for a run to the opposite side. But running the ball is not simply a surrender to the zone; it is a useful, and often necessary, way to attack it.

Quarterbacks try to dissect zones by throwing into the seams, the dead (vacant) areas where two zone areas converge. They also will try to isolate running backs one-on-one against linebackers, pass to the weakside (away from any strongside rotation), and utilize play action passes to draw in the linebackers from their coverage responsibilities.

Quarterbacks frequently attack the underneath area of the zone, the vacant underbelly that exists between the line of scrimmage and the defenders who have dropped back into their coverage areas.

As always, execution is the key to beating a

zone defense, and the passer and receiver try to time the pass to correspond with the fluctuation of the zone areas, which open and close like trap doors.

A receiver running a quick slant pattern across the middle must be aware (along with the quarterback) when he has passed the cornerback into a free area. The quarterback also must know (instinctively) when the opening has closed (when the receiver encounters a linebacker's area, for instance) and wait for another opening to occur.

The speed, reaction, and adaptive movement of cornerbacks and linebackers in response to the routes run by receivers are studied intently in the game films, in order to help cue the passer and receiver when the precious split-second openings will occur.

Then it comes down to throwing and catching the ball.

Beating Man-to-Man

The coverage men in a man-to-man defense operate on the cutting edge of disaster on nearly every pass. One false step by a cornerback or safety covering a wide receiver one-on-one can result in a disastrous big gain, or a touchdown. Receivers often can make defensive backs in a man-to-man feel very lonely.

When the bump-and-run was amended in 1977, and defenders could no longer manhandle receivers all over the field, the surest way to keep track of a receiver was to assign someone to stay with him throughout his pattern. But that is often easier said than done. The receiver (as well as the quarterback) knows exactly where he is going on a route; he also knows exactly where and when the ball should be thrown.

The defender is therefore reduced to guessing and reacting. He also is subjected to receivers who spend hours practicing to become actors—learning facial expressions, how to put on an exaggerated stride, how to dip their shoulders, all to transmit false signals to the defender. (This is why pass defenders are told to watch a receiver's belt buckle area—it goes where he goes.)

Quarterbacks often release their passes even before the receiver has moved into position to catch the ball, timing the throw so that the ball will arrive just a split second before the receiver turns to catch it (called a

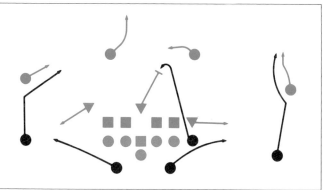

"spot pass"). That gives the defender precious little time to react to the ball in the air.

Ultimately, beating man-to-man coverage is a matter of speed, timing, and positioning. Defensive players try to hold up the receiver at the line of scrimmage as long as possible. Once the receiver breaks into his pattern, the defender tries to take away the most favorable angles in an attempt to force him out of his route, disrupting his timing. But generally with man-to-man coverage, the initiative and the advantage will almost always belong to the receiver.

Beating the Nickel

The nickel defense (and its companion, the dime) presents a problem for the offense: The addition of a fifth or sixth (dime) back into the secondary gives the defense seven or eight pass coverage men (including the linebackers responsible for pass coverage). That allows for more double teaming.

However, with five eligible receivers available on every down, someone inevitably falls into single coverage. It is the quarterback's responsibility to identify the potential double team spots before the play, which isn't easy, since one of the nickel's advantages is its ability to camouflage coverage.

Therefore, when a coach sees a nickel defense on the field, he often will recall his fullbacks who are best at blocking, along with tight ends who have trouble releasing unchecked from the line of scrimmage. In their place are put extra wide receivers (or running backs who are receiving specialists).

If the nickel is to be conquered, the offense also must use formations designed to cause the coverage to tip its hand in advance and allow accurate reads by the quarterback.

Pressuring the Quarterback

A good NFL quarterback who consistently receives ample time to get his passes away can usually shred any type of pass coverage. It is therefore imperative for the defense to mount a strong pass rush to harass the quarterback.

Three of the most popular methods of establishing a heavy pass rush are stunts, dogs, and blitzes, which widen the action, and force the blockers to deal with more space. With stunts, the offensive linemen may have to seek out their targets, which can open up space for a dogging linebacker or a looping stunt man to zero in on the quarterback.

The blitz is a great weapon when it comes as a surprise. The defense aims its blitz on the side that it expects the run or pass to go. It is used to take away a team's strength. If the offense is consistently running to the strongside, you blitz to the strongside. If the offense is sending the weakside running back out on pass patterns, the blitz goes on the weakside.

Blitzing can result in disaster, however, since the player or players involved in the blitz are deserting the pass coverage. For that reason some teams avoid blitzing, or use it only as a desperation measure; they would rather yield a succession of small gains than be beaten by a big play off a blitz mistake.

When a quarterback is sacked, it is an emotional moment for both teams; the sack invigorates the defense, while simultaneously subduing the offense's momentum—at least temporarily. Some colorful nicknames have been earned by defensive lines adept at the art of sacking quarterbacks, including the Los Angeles Rams' Fearsome Foursome, the Minnesota Vikings' Purple People Eaters, the Baltimore Colts' Sack Pack, and, most recently, the New York Jets' Sack Exchange.

Although an individual sack can inspire a defense, it can be equally effective just to apply constant pressure on the quarterback. Even if he isn't sacked, the quarterback will be forced to release the ball sooner than he may want, giving him less time to locate his primary receivers.

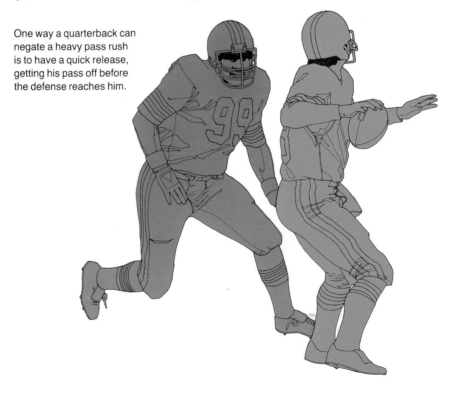

One way a quarterback can negate a heavy pass rush is to have a quick release, getting his pass off before the defense reaches him.

Slowing the Pass Rush

If the defensive ends and nose tackle in a 3-4 defense can be controlled at the line by solo blocking, the offense will storm ahead. The center wedges against the nose man, each tackle slams into an end, and the guards are free to hunt down inside linebackers. The tight end can lead the blocking on a run or enter the pattern on a pass.

However, when the rush can't be stemmed, everything changes. Extra blocking is called to the line of scrimmage. Linebackers can roam like a wolfpack, without obstruction, free to dog through the holes vacated by guards who may be sliding over to double team.

Any dog or blitz forces offensive adjustments, and multiple blitzes can make the blockers feel like pedestrians in the middle of freeway traffic.

Offenses are trained to deal with dogs and blitzes, but it requires clear thinking and split-second decisions. Of course, if a quarterback senses that a dog or blitz may be coming before the ball is snapped, he can call an audible at the line of scrimmage and switch to a play that will exploit the defensive gaps left by the blitz.

Even if the blitz comes as a surprise, the quarterback still can beat it, if he has the proper safety valves available on that play.

For instance, a running back heading out into the flat on a pass pattern will notice when the linebacker who ordinarily would be cover-

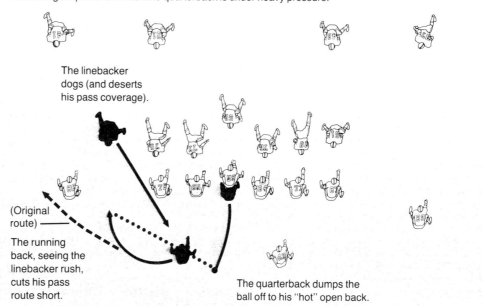

USING A SAFETY VALVE
The offense must be alert to dogs and blitzes. The running backs in particular must take immediate action to get open short when the quarterback is under heavy pressure.

The linebacker dogs (and deserts his pass coverage).

(Original route) ——

The running back, seeing the linebacker rush, cuts his pass route short.

The quarterback dumps the ball off to his "hot" open back.

ing him is blitzing instead. The back should then instinctively shorten his route, and the quarterback can dump off a pass to him, since he should be open.

Stunting, like blitzes, can create havoc with blocking schemes. Many teams "zone block" against stunts. That means the linemen stay in their areas no matter what. The tackle takes the outside rusher, whoever he is, and the guard takes the inside man.

The consequences of losing the battle at the line of scrimmage are well known to the offensive linemen. If they crumble too often in the face of the pass rush, the quarterback will have to rush his throws—increasing the odds for interceptions—and may be sacked.

Reading the Defense

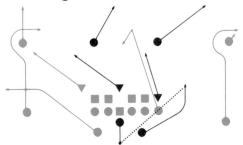

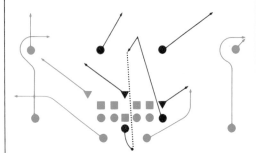

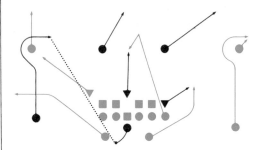

1. On this pass play against a zone defense, the quarterback reads as the safeties go into deep zones. When he sees the middle and strongside linebackers drop off into pass coverage left, he throws right to the open fullback.

2. Here, using the same play and defense as an example, the middle linebacker goes left. As the quarterback drops back, he sees the strongside linebacker come over to cover the fullback. The pass then is thrown to the tight end in the seam of the zone.

3. Again the same play and defense, but this time the quarterback sees the middle and strongside linebackers drop into pass coverage right. The quarterback responds by rolling left and hitting the wide receiver on the left.

At the line of scrimmage, the quarterback scans the defense, reading it and looking for clues to its pass coverage. Those clues then are matched against the play that has been called and the options available, ranging from switching primary receivers to changing plays altogether by calling an audible.

Sometimes a quarterback can see by where a defender lines up what he is going to do. For example, maybe the cornerback is playing up a little closer than usual, or perhaps a linebacker is trying a bit too hard to appear casual; both could mean a blitz. Or maybe a defensive back is crouched down, intently watching the receiver in front of him. That could indicate man-to-man coverage; the

back would be less concerned with just one receiver if he was going to play a zone.

Once the ball is snapped, the quarterback continues to read during his drop. He usually looks at the strong safety, whose first movements can give away a lot about the basic coverage, as can the movements of the free safety and the middle linebacker. If the two safeties, for instance, both start the same way deep, they're probably moving into zone coverage. If they divide deep, it probably indicates a double zone. If the strong safety comes up, the quarterback anticipates man-to-man.

None of this is foolproof; defenses do their best to disguise their coverages, even after

the snap. A strong safety doesn't automatically run to his zone on every play. If a receiver is headed into his area he'll take off, but if his zone isn't immediately threatened, the safety may "float" and wait. And when he doesn't make a move for his zone, the quarterback can't be sure what zone he's defending.

Pass defenders also "hide" by lining up in positions seemingly wrong for the zone they're actually assigned to cover. If the strong safety plays close to the line, he's gambling that the quarterback will not guess that he's assigned a deep zone that would be difficult, or impossible, for him to cover from that position. But if the quarterback reads intuitively, or has the right played called, the safety is in trouble.

Two-Minute Offense

Once the two-minute warning has been given, the nature and pace of a game can change dramatically. An offensive team down by two, even three scores, suddenly shifts into a "fast-forward" style of play called a two-minute offense (also called a hurry-up offense or the two-minute drill).

The clock becomes all-important and time is measured in seconds instead of minutes. The quarterback takes over. He must know, for instance, when the clock will resume on the referee's whistle. He must have his team lined up the second the play is called. He must know exactly how many time outs he has left and the proper times to use them. He must know to call for a measurement when the ball is close to a first down to afford time to call an extra play. He must forget time-consuming things such as audibles and call plays on sound or quick counts. And, he must instill in his team an attitude that winning is possible.

In fact, time becomes so vital that even the rules reflect the change; there are six rule variations for the final two minutes.

The two minute offense is not a separate set of plays designed exclusively for quick scores when a team is behind. Rather, it is the day's game plan condensed and streamlined.

Because the clock will not stop after an in-bounds running play, the ground game in a two-minute offense is all but shut down. Straight ahead power plays for short-yardage first downs may be left in. So might some influence plays, traps, and draws for exploiting a defense overcommitted against the lifeblood of the two-minute offense—the pass.

Defenses, concerned with keeping the clock moving and protecting against a quick strike, counter the two-minute offense by moving into a "prevent" formation. In a prevent, defenses weaken themselves against the run—almost inviting it—by taking out one lineman in favor of an extra linebacker or defensive back. (In a 3-4, linebackers are shifted with, or exchanged for, defensive backs.) Generally, two deep backs are deployed far behind their normal stations, while others inch toward the sidelines, guarding against the sideline patterns by which an offense can stop the clock without using a time out. Linebackers retreat

Shula on the Two-Minute Offense:
"You take what the defense gives in the last two minutes. You're going to get hurt trying to force it into that soft defense. But if you take the shorter stuff, you hope that, say, the running back who catches a pass can break a tackle. When that happens, five- or six-yard gains turn into seventeen or eighteen yarders."

deeper than at other times, further reducing the defense's ability to stop the run.

As a result, the quarterback sees a wider, longer blanket of coverage, concentrated deep and near the sidelines. This opens up the middle of the field, underneath the coverage, and that's where most quarterbacks try to beat the prevent defense. The quarterback can't stop the clock (except by calling a time out) with a pass over the middle. But he might compensate with a much more substantial gain. In essence, what he's trying to do to a prevent defense is stretch it beyond its ability to snap back. This is done by pushing the edges of the defense outward, using wide receivers as deep decoys, then throwing to the tight end or a running back cutting across the middle of the field. Another method is to flood one side of the formation, or even better, the deep secondary, with receivers, which forces the defense to cover larger areas of the field, causing gaps and coverage break downs.

The Rules

The Official Rules for Professional Football is a 131-page publication divided into 18 sections that cover everything from the dimensions of the playing field to the handling of emergencies. Only a select few men are completely conversant with the book's contents, and they are NFL officials and league personnel.

The NFL employs 107 officials. They are broken down into 15 seven-man crews—referee, umpire, line judge, head linesman, back judge, side judge, and field judge—and two swing officials. Fourteen of the crews have one week off during the season; the other has two weeks.

Crews are established by the third week of the preseason and work together through the completion of the regular season. In establishing the crews, the league seeks an equal balance of experience and ability. There will never be more than one rookie per crew.

All officials are paid $300 for preseason games. The regular season rate ranges from $325 a game (first- and second-year men) to $800 (for officials with 11 years experience). Playoff game assignments are worth $2,000. The Super Bowl pays $3,000. The AFC-NFC Pro Bowl pays $1,000.

Unlike the players, an official has responsibilities on every play in a game. There are more than 3,000 plays each season when his judgement must be precise. He must be capable of calling to mind instantly even the most obscure rules. When he does his job best, he does it in anonymity, a man in black and white in a theater of color.

Every play and every call undergo intense scrutiny. Each official is rated by the two head coaches in the game he works, a league observer assigned to the game, and by Art McNally, NFL supervisor of officials, and his staff when they review the game films, which are supplied by the home team.

The rating system is seven (excellent) through one (unsatisfactory) and is applied to areas of judgement, game control, position and coverge, reaction under pressure, and decisiveness. Through composite ratings a cumulative total is compiled over the season. The highest-rated officials at each position earn the postseason assignments.

"When you combine our ratings with what the coaches offer and what our observer has seen, we feel we have about as comprehensive a report as possible," says McNally.

It takes McNally and his staff approximately six hours to review a single game film. The process starts in New York Tuesday morning and is completed—for all 14 games—by Thursday afternoon at 4:00. When the reports are completed, a copy of the game film, a detailed critique of every play, and an evaluation of each call are shipped to the site of the crew's next game.

Officials are required to be at their assigned city by 6:00 P.M. the day before the game. They meet to review the film and analyze the league's critique and evaluation. The process takes anywhere from two-and-a-half to three hours.

NFL officials are professionals on and off the field. During the week they function in jobs ranging from teachers to business executives. On the weekends their business is pro football. Their average age is 49 and the average overall officiating experience is 24 years (the average NFL officiating experience is 9.4 years).

They have gone through a demanding process to earn their NFL stripes.

"We want a man who has officiated a minimum of ten years, five at the college level," says McNally. "He must belong to an accredited association. He takes intelligence and psychological tests and undergoes a three-hour interview by a professional service.

"This is followed by in-depth security checks and extensive meetings with members of our staff. We want to find out all we can about our men."

Once in the NFL fold, officials are constantly required to review the rules; the job always is a learning process. During the season they have the films, critiques, and evaluations. In the offseason they receive a film from Mc-

Nally that covers every call the particular official made (or didn't make) during the previous season. Officials also complete a comprehensive rules review that includes an open-book test, and in July they attend a week-long clinic.

The rules the officials enforce have been established and approved by the 28 NFL club presidents, who get input from the four-man NFL Competition Committee. The committee is charged with evaluating everything relative to the competition of professional football.

The four men—Paul Brown, vice president and general manager of the Cincinnati Bengals; Eddie LeBaron, executive vice president and chief operating officer of the Atlanta Falcons; Tex Schramm, president and general manager of the Dallas Cowboys; and Don Shula, vice president and head coach of the Miami Dolphins—have 108 years of combined experience in the NFL as either players, coaches, or administrators. They meet each year for a two-week period prior to the annual team owners meeting.

The items on the rules portion of the agenda come from a variety of sources. Clubs are required to submit formal proposals for new rules or rule changes to the NFL office by January 31. These are automatically presented to the owners for a vote.

Any other suggested changes—which come from fans, media, and officials—are brought to the committee's attention if they are found to have merit.

After the changes or new rules have cleared the committee, they are formally submitted to the owners for a vote. The presentation includes the committee's opinion on the proposal, which may or may not influence the balloting. According to the NFL Constitution and By-Laws, playing rules may be amended or changed by a vote of at least 21 of the 28 club presidents.

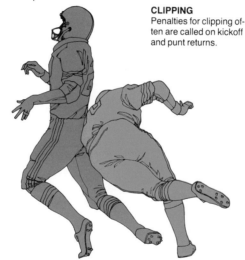

CLIPPING
Penalties for clipping often are called on kickoff and punt returns.

Official Terms

A basic understanding of what is and isn't legal can make the game more entertaining.

First, some important definitions, taken alphabetically for easy reference.

Chucking is the warding off of an opponent who is in front of a defender by contacting him with a quick extension of the arm or arms, followed by the return of the arm(s) to a flexed position, thereby breaking the original contact.

Clipping is throwing the body across the back of an opponent's leg(s) or hitting him from the back while moving up from behind. A ball carrier cannot be clipped. Clipping is legal in close line play, which is the area between the positions normally occupied by the offensive tackles, extending three yards on each side of the line of scrimmage.

Encroachment is when a player is in the neutral zone at the time of the snap or makes contact with an opponent before the ball is snapped.

A **fair catch** is an unhindered catch of a kick (including a kickoff) by a member of the receiving team, who must raise one arm the full length above his head while the kick is in flight.

Offside is when any part of the player's body is beyond his scrimmage or free kick line when the ball is snapped.

Pass blocking is the obstruction of an opponent by the use of that part of the body above the knees. During a legal block, open or closed hands must be inside the blocker's elbows and can be thrust forward to contact an opponent as long as the contact is inside the frame, which is defined as that part of the opponent's body below the neck that is presented to the blocker. The blocker cannot use his hands to push from behind, hang onto, or encircle the opponent. Use of the hands usually results in holding penalties.

Possession is control of the ball. When a player catches a forward pass, he must control the ball throughout the act of clearly touching both feet, or any part of his body other than his hands, to the ground inbounds.

A **return kick** is a kick made by a kicker after team possession has changed during a down. Any number of return kicks may be made (but rarely are) on one down (i.e., Team A kicks to Team B, which in return, kicks to Team A, ad infinitum).

Run blocking is an aggressive action by a blocker to obstruct an opponent from the ball carrier. During a legal block, contact can be made with the head, shoulders, hands, and/or outer surface of the forearm, or any other part of the body. Hands, with extended arms, cannot be used to contact an opponent either inside or outside the opponent's frame. The blocker cannot use his hands, arms, or legs to grasp, trip, hang onto, or encircle an opponent to gain an advantage.

A **shift** is the movement of two or more offensive players at the same time before the snap.

A **touchback** occurs when a ball is dead on or behind the team's own goal line, provided the impetus came from an opponent and provided it is not a touchdown. The ball is put into play on the receiving (or defensive) team's 20 yard line.

Starting and Stopping the Clock

Unless otherwise specified, halftimes are 15 minutes. Teams do not necessarily have to leave the field at halftime, but they always do.

Each team is allowed three charged time outs of 90 seconds each half. A team cannot call consecutive charged time outs.

On kickoffs in the final two minutes of each half, the clock does not start until the ball has been legally touched by either team in the field of play. In all other cases, the clock starts with the kickoff.

Following all changes of possession, the clock starts running when the ball is snapped.

It is an automatic referee's time out when the player who originally takes the snap is tackled behind the line of scrimmage. The clock starts as soon as the ball has been spotted for the succeeding down. If the player who takes the snap obviously makes no effort to advance beyond the line, the officials are instructed not to stop the clock.

A half or game cannot end on a defensive penalty. On a foul by the defense on the last play of the half or game, the down is replayed if the penalty is accepted. Offensive fouls that occur at the end of a half or game do not extend the period.

Players, Substitutes, Equipment

Each team is permitted no more than 11 men on the field at the time of the snap; a five yard penalty is called for 12 or more. There is no penalty for fewer than 11 men on the field.

Players wearing numbers not qualifying them for designated positions (such as a tackle playing the third tight end in a short-yardage situation) must report their change to the referee prior to the huddle. The referee is responsible for notifyng the defensive captain of the change.

The use of adhesive or slippery substances on the body, equipment, or uniform of any player is illegal.

All players must wear a helmet with a chin strap fastened, shoulder pads, hip pads, thigh pads, knee pads, stockings, and acceptable shoes (barefoot kicking is permissible).

The name of each player must be attached to his jersey.

Tearaway jerseys are illegal.

Face masks cannot be made of lucite, clear plastic, or a similar material.

Kickoffs

Kickoffs occur from the kicking team's 35 yard line at the start of each half and following extra points and successful field goal attempts.

All players on the receiving team of a punt or kickoff are prohibited from blocking below the waist.

A kickoff is illegal unless it travels 10 yards or is touched by the receiving team. Once the ball has traveled 10 yards and/or is touched by the receiving team it is a free ball. The receiver may recover and advance the ball. The kicking team may recover but not advance it unless the receiver had possession and lost the ball (a fumble).

When a kickoff goes out of bounds between the goal lines without being touched by the receiving team, it must be kicked again (after assessment of a five-yard penalty).

When a kickoff goes out of bounds between the goal lines and is touched last by the receiving team, it is the receiving team's ball at the out of bounds spot.

When a kickoff travels beyond the receiving team's end zone, or is downed by a player on the receiving team in the end zone, it is ruled a touchback.

Kicks From Scrimmage (Punts and Field Goals)

Any punt or missed field goal that touches a goal post is dead.

During a punt or field goal, only the end men, as eligible receivers on the line of scrimmage at the time of the snap, are permitted to go beyond the line of scrimmage before the ball is kicked.

Any punt that is blocked and does not cross the line of scrimmage can be recovered and advanced by either team (the kicking team can run the ball or throw a pass). However, if the kicking (offensive) team recovers the ball, it must make the necessary yardage for its first down to retain possession if the punt was on fourth down.

The defensive team may advance all kicks from scrimmage whether or not the ball has crossed the line of scrimmage.

The kicking team may never advance its own kick if legal recovery is made *beyond* the line of scrimmage.

A member of the receiving team may not run into or rough a kicker who kicks from behind his line unless the contact (1) is incidental to and after he had touched the ball in flight (deflected or blocked), (2) is caused by the kicker's own motions (such as moving around to avoid the rush), or (3) occurs during a quick kick, or after a kicker recovers a loose ball (the ball is loose when the kicker muffs the snap or the snap hits the ground).

Any member of the punting team may down the ball anywhere in the field of play.

If a member of the kicking team attempts to down the ball on or inside the opponent's 5 yard line and carries the ball into the end zone, it is a touchback.

It is illegal for a defensive player to jump or stand on any player or to use a hand or hands on a teammate to gain additional height or leverage in an attempt to block a kick.

A player can punt the ball from anywhere in the field of play, including beyond the line of scrimmage. On kicks beyond the line, all rules pertaining to ineligible men downfield and running into the kicker no longer apply.

On missed field goals from a scrimmage line beyond the 20 yard line, the ball goes to the defensive team at the scrimmage line. A missed field goal from a scrimmage line inside the 20 yard line will result in the defense taking possession of the ball at the 20.

Extra Points

The defensive team can never score on an extra point attempt.

Any foul committed on a successful extra point will be assessed on the ensuing kickoff.

Free Kick After a Fair Catch

On a free kick after a fair catch, the captain of the receiving team must decide whether his team will put the ball in play by a punt, dropkick, placekick without a tee, or by snap. If the placekick or dropkick goes between the uprights it is a field goal.

Fair Catch

A player who signals for a fair catch is not required to catch the ball. However, if the player makes the fair catch signal, he may not block or initiate contact with any player on the kicking team until the ball touches a player.

If the ball hits the ground, or touches a member of the kicking team while it is in flight, the fair catch signal is off.

Any undue advance of the ball by a receiver who has signaled and made a fair catch is delay of game.

Receivers can make a fair catch in the end zone. If the ball is caught it is a touchback.

Position of Players at the Snap

The offensive team must have at least seven players on the line. With the exception of the quarterback, all offensive players not on the line must be at least one yard back at the snap.

No interior linemen (tackle to tackle) may move after taking or simulating a three-point stance.

All players on the offensive team must be stationary at the snap, except for one player who may be in motion parallel to or backward from the line of scrimmage.

After a shift or huddle, all players on the offensive team must come to an absolute stop for at least one second.

Quarterbacks can be called for a false start penalty if their actions, including their cadence, are judged to be an obvious attempt to draw an opponent offside.

Use of Hands, Arms, and Body

No player on offense may assist a runner except by blocking for him. A runner may ward off opponents with his hands and arms, but no other player on offense may use his hands or arms to obstruct an opponent by grasping with his hands, pushing, or encircling any part of his body during a block. In summary, you can't hold another player or push your running back forward in an attempt to gain yardage.

A defensive player cannot contact an opponent above the shoulders with the palm of his hand except to ward him off the line. The head slap is illegal.

A defensive player may not tackle or hold an opponent other than a runner or passer.

Five-Yard Contact Rule

The advent of the five-yard contact rule in 1978 radically affected the bump and run technique most commonly used by defensive backs. Receivers think it is a great rule; defenders don't like it at all. An eligible receiver is considered to be an "obstructing opponent" only to a point five yards beyond the line of scrimmage unless the quarterback who receives the snap clearly demonstrates no further intention to pass. Within this five-yard zone, a defensive player may make contact with an eligible receiver that may be maintained as long as it is continuous and unbroken. Beyond this five-yard limitation, the defender may use his hands or arms only to defend or protect himself against impending contact caused by a receiver.

Crackbacks

An offensive player who lines up more than two yards outside his own tackle, or a player who, at the snap, is in a backfield position and subsequently takes a position more than two yards outside the tackle, may not clip an opponent anywhere, nor may he contact an opponent below the waist if the blocker is moving toward the ball (a crackback) and if the con-

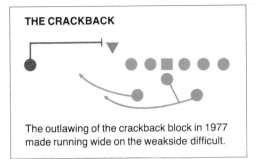

THE CRACKBACK

The outlawing of the crackback block in 1977 made running wide on the weakside difficult.

tact is made within an area five yards on either side of the line.

Forward Pass

A forward pass may be touched or caught by any eligible receiver. Eligible receivers on offense are players on either end of the line of scrimmage or players at least one yard behind the line at the snap. A T-formation quarterback is not eligible to receive a forward pass; Shotgun formation quarterbacks are.

All members of the defensive team are eligible to intercept a pass.

An offensive team may make only one forward pass during each play, provided that the ball has not crossed the line of scrimmage. A legal forward pass must be thrown from behind the line of scrimmage. If the passer crosses the line, then retreats behind it and throws a pass, it is illegal. Illegal passes, however, can be intercepted.

Any offensive player may throw a forward

pass. If the pass is touched by one offensive player and then is caught by a second eligible offensive player, the pass completion is legal. This is a rule amended in 1978. Because of it, every NFL team now has tip play passes in its playbook (see page 50). The offensive players are not allowed to tip the ball toward the goal line. The direction must be parallel to the goal line or the rear of the receiver. All offensive players become eligible receivers once a pass is touched by an eligible receiver or any defensive player.

If a forward pass is caught simultaneously by eligible players on opposing teams, possession goes to the passing team.

Any pass that hits the goal post or crossbar is a dead ball.

A forward pass is complete when a receiver clearly touches the ground with both feet inbounds while in possession of the ball. If the receiver clearly is pushed out of bounds while in possession in the air, the pass is complete at the out of bounds spot.

If a receiver steps out of bounds and then returns to the field to catch a pass, the pass is incomplete.

Protection of the Passer

A pass begins when the passer—with possession of the ball—starts to bring his hand forward. If the ball strikes the ground after this action has begun, the pass is ruled incomplete. If the passer loses control of the ball prior to

bringing his hand forward, the play is ruled a fumble. On plays from scrimmage, referees position themselves to the throwing side of the quarterback to get a better angle on this type of situation.

No defensive player may run into a passer of a legal forward pass after the ball has left the passer's hand. The referee must make a judgement on whether or not the opponent has a reasonable chance to stop his momentum while the passer still has the ball.

The referee is to blow the play dead as soon as he makes the judgement that the quarterback is clearly in the grasp and control of a tackler.

Pass Interference

Pass interference occurs when any player's movement beyond the line of scrimmage hinders the progress of an eligible opponent in his attempt to reach a pass. Incidental contact when two or more eligible players make a simultaneous and bona fide attempt to catch or bat the ball is permitted. If they play the ball—not the man—it is not interference. Defensive players have as much right to the ball as eligible receivers.

It is extremely important to understand that the restrictions for pass interference begin for the passing team with the snap, and for the defense when the ball leaves the passer's hand. Both restrictions end when the ball is touched by anyone. An example: The tight end runs a

pattern up the middle of the field and makes contact with the strong safety, knocking him to the ground. Meanwhile, the quarterback has been forced to scramble out of the pocket by the pass rush; he eventually finds the wide receiver alone in the end zone for a touchdown. As the catch is being made a penalty

PASS INTERFERENCE
Offensive receivers and pass defenders have an equal right to the ball, but neither can interfere with the other's attempt to make a catch.

flag is seen floating through the air. The call is offensive pass interference on the tight end (the restrictions begin for the offense when the ball is snapped).

Pass interference rules are not considered in effect on passes thrown to receivers who are behind the line of scrimmage.

Intentional Grounding

Intentional grounding is when, in the judgement of the referee, the passer purposely throws the ball away to prevent a loss of yardage.

Backward Pass

A pass parallel to the line is a backward pass (also called a lateral). A runner may toss the ball backward at any time. Any player on either team may catch the pass or recover the ball after it touches the ground.

A backward pass that strikes the ground can be recovered and advanced by the offensive team.

A backward pass that strikes the ground can be recovered but cannot be advanced by the defensive team (remember that the snap is a backward pass). If the defense catches the backward pass while it is in the air, it can advance the ball.

Fumble-Muff

The distinction between a fumble and a muff is important. A fumble implies possession; a muff does not. A fumble may be advanced by any player on either team regardless of whether it is recovered before or after the ball hits the ground. The defense cannot advance a muff unless it is recovered before the ball hits the ground.

If a loose ball goes out of bounds, the last team having possession on that play retains possession.

Fourth-Down Fumble

If an offensive player fumbles anywhere on the field during a fourth-down play, or if a player fumbles on any down after the two-minute warning in a half, only the fumbling player is permitted to recover and/or advance the ball. If the ball is recovered by any other offensive player, the ball is dead at the spot of the fumble unless it is recovered behind the spot of the fumble (the ball is then dead at the spot of the recovery). The defensive team can recover and advance the ball as always.

Penalty Options

When a penalty is called, the non-penalized team usually has the option to accept or decline it. (Some penalties carry automatic assessments.) The decision to accept or decline a penalty, made by the non-penalized team's captain, is a strategic one based on which choice will prove more beneficial given the situation. An example: On a third-and-inches play from the 50, the offense is stopped for no gain *and* called offside (a five-yard penalty). The defense then has the option to accept the penalty and allow the offense to play third down over from five yards back (and giving them another chance to make a first down). Or, the defense can decline the penalty, making it fourth down, and force the offense into a certain punting situation. The obvious choice is to decline. If there are equivalent penalties called against both teams *on the same play*, the referee normally will rule *offsetting* penalties and the down will be replayed.

Odds and Ends

Teams are allowed to designate two captains per unit (offense, defense, special teams). Only the designated captains can call time outs. Only one captain is permitted to indicate the team's choice of penalty options. His first choice stands.

The forward part of the ball in its position when declared dead in the field of play is used as the determining point in measuring any distance gained. The ball is not rotated when measuring.

Players who spike the ball while the clock is running are penalized for delay of game.

No offensive player may push a runner or lift him to his feet.

If the momentum of making an interception inside the defense's 5 yard line carries the defensive player and the ball into the end zone, the ball is next put in play at the spot of the interception unless the interceptor advances it into the field of play.

Summary of Penalties
Automatic First Down

1. Awarded to the offensive team on all defensive fouls with these exceptions: offside, encroachment, delay of game, illegal substitutions, excessive timeout(s), and incidental grasp of the face mask.

Loss of Down (no yardage)

1. Second forward pass behind the line.
2. Forward pass strikes ground, goal post, or crossbar.
3. Forward pass goes out of bounds.
4. Forward pass is first touched by eligible receiver who has gone out of bounds and returned.
5. Forward pass accidentally touches ineligible receiver on or behind line.
6. Forward pass thrown from behind line of scrimmage after ball crossed the line.

Five Yards

1. Crawling.
2. Defensive holding or illegal use of hands (automatic first down).
3. Delay of game.
4. Encroachment.
5. Too many time outs.
6. False start.
7. Illegal formation.
8. Illegal shift.
9. Illegal motion.
10. Illegal substitution.
11. Kickoff out of bounds between goal lines that is not touched.
12. Invalid fair catch signal.
13. More than 11 players on the field at the snap for either team.
14. Less than seven men on the offensive line at the snap.
15. Offside.
16. Failure to pause one second after a shift or huddle.
17. Running into kicker (automatic first down).
18. More than one man in motion at snap.
19. Grasping face mask of opponent.
20. Player out of bounds at snap.
21. Ineligible member(s) of kicking team going beyond line of scrimmage before the ball is kicked.
22. Illegal return.
23. Failure to report a change of eligibility.
24. Helping the runner.

10 Yards

1. Offensive pass interference.
2. Ineligible player downfield during passing down.
3. Holding, illegal use of hands by the offense.
4. Tripping by a member of either team.

15 Yards

1. Clipping.
2. Fair catch interference.
3. Illegal batting or punching of loose ball.
4. Deliberately kicking a loose ball.
5. Illegal crackback block by the offense.
6. Piling on a ball carrier (automatic first down).
7. Roughing the kicker (automatic first down).
8. Roughing the passer (automatic first down).
9. Twisting, turning, or pulling an opponent's face mask.
10. Unnecessary roughness.
11. Unsportsmanlike conduct.
12. Delay of game at the start of either half.
13. Illegal blocking below the waist.

Five Yards and Loss of Down

1. Forward pass thrown from *beyond* the line of scrimmage.

10 Yards and Loss of Down

1. Intentional grounding of a forward pass (safety if the passer is in his end zone).

15 Yards and Loss of Coin Toss Option

1. Team's late arrival on the field prior to the scheduled kickoff.

15 Yards (and disqualification if flagrant)

1. Striking an opponent with a fist.
2. Kicking or kneeing an opponent.
3. Striking an opponent on head or neck with forearm, elbow, or hands.
4. Roughing the kicker.
5. Roughing the passer.
6. Malicious unnecessary roughness.
7. Unsportsmanlike conduct.
8. Palpably unfair act. (It is a distance penalty determined by the referee after consultation with other officials.)

Suspension From Game

1. Illegal equipment. (The player may return after one down when legally equipped.)

Touchdown

1. When the referee determines a palpably unfair act deprived a team of a touchdown. (Example: a player comes off the bench and tackles a runner apparently en route to a touchdown.)

Behind the Scenes

There is more to an NFL football team than pulling linemen, weakside rotations, and play action passes.

The players and coaches usually receive all the glory (or criticism) from fans and the press, but the real "roster" of an NFL club extends greatly beyond the 45-player squad and the coaches on the sideline.

A successful NFL franchise must be a smoothly functioning operation, from the highest levels of the front office to the ushers in the stadium. It is the year-round, behind the scenes activity of a team's administrative personnel that ultimately can determine how successful it will be. For, just as all NFL teams employ different strategies on the football field, each club also has a distinctive approach to its off-the-field operations.

Beginning with the very top level of administration, there are several different forms of team ownership in the NFL. Some franchises are owned outright by one individual. Others are private corporations, or partnerships with one partner serving as operating head of the club. One club, the Green Bay Packers, is a publicly owned franchise that is supported by stockholders and governed by an executive committee chosen by a 45-man board of directors.

The owners are the governing power in the NFL. Though the league is run on a day-to-day basis by its office in New York, which is directed by a commissioner (who is selected by the owners), all major decisions affecting the league or the sport itself must be brought before the owners for approval.

The degree of involvement by an NFL owner or owners varies, but usually the overall direction of a club's football operation falls within the domain of a president, vice president, or general manager. On some clubs, the head coach also serves as general manager, but in most cases the jobs are held by two different people.

As the club's chief administrator, the operating head usually becomes involved with nearly every aspect of the team's operation. But pro football has become an elaborate sport, and virtually every NFL front office employs full-time professionals in the following areas: player personnel, scouting, public relations, finance, marketing, ticket sales, equipment, medicine, stadium management, and, with increasing frequency, computer programming.

Among a typical vice president's or general manager's responsibilities are the final decisions on all trades, draft selections, and other personnel moves; player contract negotiations; interaction with other NFL teams and the league office; and the effective blending of all of the components of the franchise into an efficient organization.

The most visible administrative position on an NFL club almost always is the head coach. He receives the credit (usually) when the team wins; he also receives the criticism when the team loses.

An NFL head coach must possess a number of varied skills. He has to exhibit leadership. He must be an effective teacher. Since he performs so often in the public eye, he must possess outstanding communicative and public relations skills. At times the coach must play the role of psychologist. He has to be able to motivate his players and his staff. He must delegate authority efficiently. He has to be able to "think on his feet," and make quick decisions in the heat of action. And he must be able to cope with the extraordinary pressures that are part of the job.

A team's strategy on the field originates with the head coach and his staff, and a team's personality subsequently reflects the philosophies of its coaching staff.

The increased emphasis on specialization in the NFL has led to a greater dependency on assistant coaches, and there has been a corresponding swelling in the ranks of assistants. For instance, in 1971 the Philadelphia Eagles had 6 assistant coaches; 10 years later they had 11.

Most teams now have offensive and/or defensive coordinators, or an assistant head coach, who are responsible for implementing strategy for either the offense or the defense. A head coach can't afford to become *too* detached from either the offense or the defense (and some head coaches take direct responsibility for either one or the other themselves). But the presence of offensive and defensive coordinators frees the head coach to spend more time in the overall direction of the team.

Nearly every club has separate full-time coaches to handle the offensive line, the offensive backfield, the receivers, the defensive line, the linebackers, and the defensive backs. Some teams also have a coach exclusively for the quarterbacks. Many teams also have just one coach to coordinate the special teams. A rising number of teams are hiring strength and conditioning coaches. And a few clubs have identified a need for purely administrative coaching aides, who assist with the analysis of film and other off-the-field functions. (At least two NFL clubs have a coach whose primary responsibility is research.)

One of the single greatest factors that can affect the outcome of a game, or even a season, is injury. Therefore, one of the unsung heroes and one of the most crucial "behind the scenes" people on an NFL club is the head trainer.

Because football is a contact sport, involving injuries of nearly every degree, all NFL clubs enlist the services of one or more medical doctors, often on a consulting basis.

But the trainer, who usually is a licensed physical therapist, is the one person who most significantly molds the overall health of a team from day-to-day, both during the season and in the offseason.

Identifying the severity of an injury always is paramount for a trainer. Some players would try to play on a broken leg (some even have!). Other players, whose thresholds for pain may not be so great, need prodding from the trainer to ignore relatively minor injuries in order to play.

Sometimes there is a fine line between being hurt and being injured. It is up to the trainer to recognize when an injury is serious enough to warrant further examination by a doctor.

Like a head coach, a trainer must be a part-time psychologist. He has to work with injured players throughout the rehabilitation process and he must be someone in whom the players have complete trust.

The health of an NFL franchise also is very much in the hands of some other front office professionals. The public relations office helps foster a team's image, in part by its relationship with the press. The sale of tickets—vital to every team's financial well-being—must be expertly coordinated by the ticket manager and his staff. The scouting and personnel departments must be staffed by people who can sense talent in young players and know how it should be developed. The equipment manager is responsible for the acquisition, upkeep, transport, and replacement of an elaborate collection of football gear. And the marketing or promotions department helps stimulate interest in the team both locally and nationally.

Filling Out The Roster

Naturally, you can't play the game without the players. Therefore, the decision-making process of a club's personnel department is one of the most important keys to its success.

Every NFL club is allowed to carry 45 players on its active roster during the regular season. That number has fluctuated through the years. In 1925, for instance, the number of players an NFL team could have was only 16.

Clubs are permitted to open their pre-season training camps with an unlimited number of players, but, thereafter, each club must comply with a series of mandatory roster reductions in order to reach the 45-man limit the week prior to the regular season opener.

There are four basic methods of acquiring players in the NFL. A club can draft players during the league's annual college selection meeting in the spring; it can sign players who are free agents; it can claim players who have been put on waivers; and it can trade for players.

Every NFL club tries to construct its player foundation through successful drafting. But the acquisition of players through trades, free agency, and waivers also are valuable methods of fulfilling specific position needs and attaining necessary depth.

Trades provide the most interesting avenue for obtaining players. Sometimes there is controversy involved; always there is a gamble.

Certain guidelines imposed by the league office govern trading in the NFL. All trades must be submitted to—and approved by—the league, and no trades can be conducted after the completion of the sixth week of the regular season until the conclusion of the Super Bowl.

But the rest of the time clubs are free to shop around for any player deals that might help their teams. Multi-player trades are rarities; teams today are more inclined to barter with draft choices, if at all.

A less risky method of acquiring a player is through the NFL's waiver system. If a team places a player on waivers, the other 27 clubs either file claims to obtain the player or waive the opportunity to do so. Claiming clubs are assigned players on a priority basis, based on the inverse of won-lost standings. The claiming period normally is 10 days during the offseason and 24 hours from early July through December.

In some cases, another 24 hours is added on to allow the original club to rescind its action (known as a recall of a waiver request) and/or the claiming club to do the same (known as a withdrawal of a claim). If a player passes through waivers unclaimed and is not recalled by the original club, he becomes a free agent and is eligible to try to sign with any club of his choosing. All waivers from July through December are no-recall and no-withdrawal. Also, a veteran with at least four years service may have the option to reject a waiver assignment and become a free agent.

NFL clubs always are on the lookout for attractive free agents, because every year, a few undrafted free agents, or free agents who have been cut or waived by another team, emerge from nowhere to become stars.

Occasionally during the offseason, a club may sponsor a "pay your own way" free agent tryout session (one club calls its tryouts "The Gong Show") in hopes of discovering a diamond in the rough, or a player who fits in with its system or style of play, even if he has failed elsewhere.

In this age of increasingly sophisticated scouting and scientific drafting, however, the number of "unknown" players dwindles with each successive year.

Scouting and the Draft

Because the NFL draft provides such a wonderful opportunity for a club to cycle young talent onto its roster, it is essential for each club to engage in an exhaustive search for top college prospects. This is called scouting. Nearly every NFL team supplements its own scouting efforts by being part of a scouting combine. A scouting combine provides statistical and subjective input on virtually every top college football player in the country to each of the teams belonging to the combine. The two largest scouting combines are BLESTO, which serves 7 NFL clubs, and UNITED, which has 16 clubs.

The talent hunters for the scouting combines now do much of the leg work that had to be accomplished by each club individually in the past. But because every club has specific needs from each annual draft, and because clubs invariably are looking for different types of players, the braintrust on the NFL club in the end determines its own fate in the draft.

A typical NFL club can view (either in person or on film) and compile reports on as many as 2,000 college players for a single draft. A top prospect often can be the subject of between 8 to 12 reports—from different sources—just for one team.

Prospects are commonly rated on the following critical factors: (1) character; (2) quickness and control; (3) competitiveness; (4) mental alertness; and (5) strength and explosion. Of course, the non-subjective "measurables" that have been used for decades are height, weight, and speed in the 40-yard dash.

All clubs are involved in pooled timing and testing sessions of the top 150 draft-eligible players in late winter and early spring. These sessions include careful physical examinations by all the club doctors.

Very few players are considered "sure things," so there always is a great deal of thoughtful analysis given to the draft. Some of the greatest players in college football history have been flops in the NFL. Conversely, players with little better than mediocre college backgrounds, or players who came from little-known schools, and even some athletes who didn't play college football at all, have gone on to star in the NFL. But the backgrounds of its draft choices notwithstanding, every team knows that several bad drafts in a row can be extremely harmful, and that a good draft sometimes can immediately lift a club into playoff contention.

The NFL draft is held on or about May 1. It consists of 12 rounds of selections that span a two-day period.

The drafting order is set in inverse order of the teams' standing in the league. In other words, the team with the poorest record drafts first, and so on. The winner of the Super Bowl drafts last, and the Super Bowl loser drafts twenty-seventh, regardless of record. The other playoff teams with equal records move down in the order depending on how they fared in postseason play.

Once drafted by an NFL club, a player is prohibited from signing with any other NFL club unless he is traded, released, or assigned through the waiver system by the club that originally drafted him.

Most clubs generally try to draft the "best available athlete" when it is their turn to select. However, if a club has a dire need at a particular position, it will sometimes compromise on the "best available athlete" credo in order to fill its void.

The talent of some years is considered to be leaner than in others. Consequently, teams occasionally will stockpile draft choices by trading some of their selections in a lean year for similar or even higher choices in a future draft. There often is a flurry of trade activity just prior to the draft, as clubs jockey for the drafting position that will allow them the best chances of acquiring the early round choices they want.

If a college player loses his eligibility after the completion of the NFL draft, a supplemental draft is conducted. In the same order as the previous draft (the club with the worst record chooses first), each club has the opportunity to sacrifice its first pick in the next regular draft to select the athlete. The process continues until the player is selected. Non-drafted players can be signed after the draft.

Uniforms and Equipment

Once a team has its players, it must equip them. And equipping an NFL team can be a challenging, not to mention expensive, task.

The most visible portion of a player's "equipment" is his uniform. Uniforms help give a team its personality. They also bond the play-ers on a team in a special fraternity that ties the wearers to a past tradition.

For the most part, NFL teams are free to choose their own uniform colors and designs. There are certain uniform standards established by the league, however, and compliance is monitored by NFL observers at every game.

All NFL teams are required to have one set of colored jerseys and one set of white jerseys. At one time the league rule stated that the home team would wear colored jerseys and the visiting team would wear white. Now the rule is that the home team has first choice.

Some superstitions have inevitably developed regarding the success a team has in either its colored or its white jerseys. As a result, some interesting psychological dramas have been played out over the choice of uniform colors.

Some NFL coaches always prefer to have their teams play in the all white uniforms because of a longstanding belief that players appear larger in white.

There is sometimes even a strategy behind the *size* of a uniform jersey. Offensive linemen often will wear jerseys that are actually too small for them so that the fit is skin tight. The reason? Defensive linemen won't have anything to grab onto. And now that pass blockers are allowed to use their hands more while protecting the quarterback, defensive linemen have become more conscious of wearing tight fitting uniform jerseys as well.

The design of a team's helmet also has been used to gain an edge. In 1978, the New York Jets changed uniforms and went from white to green helmets, so that they would be the only team in the AFC Eastern Division that didn't wear white. They thought the green helmets would prove advantageous to a quarterback trying to pick out receivers.

Footwear has changed right along with helmets and jerseys. The advent of artificial playing surfaces has resulted in new types of footwear for NFL players. There is a different kind of shoe for every surface, and every NFL player is equipped with a variety of shoe/surface options.

Gloves also are a part of some players' equipment. Offensive linemen wear thick, heavy gloves to protect their fingers from the rigors of line play. Wide receivers and tight ends sometimes wear thin gloves on cold days to keep their hands warm.

Underneath the colorful uniform jerseys and pants there is another uniform: a layer of protective equipment that has been designed and upgraded through the years to help prevent injury. The NFL also has standards that require all players to wear the same basic padding.

Shoulder pads, elbow pads, hip pads, thigh pads, and knee pads are all part of an NFL player's armor, in addition to his jockstrap, mouthpiece, and helmet.

NFL PROTECTIVE EQUIPMENT

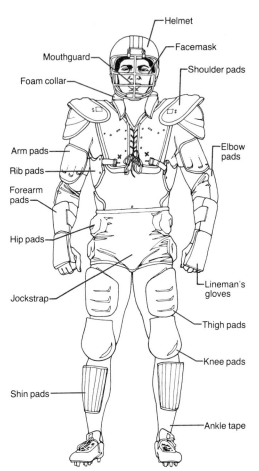

Helmet
Facemask
Mouthguard
Shoulder pads
Foam collar
Arm pads
Elbow pads
Rib pads
Forearm pads
Hip pads
Lineman's gloves
Jockstrap
Thigh pads
Knee pads
Shin pads
Ankle tape

A player's most important piece of equipment is his helmet. Football helmets have undergone dramatic evolution, from the flimsy leather headgear worn in pro football's early days to the energy absorbing, plastic helmets of the space age that contain air cells or liquid to lessen the effects of shock. New helmet designs constantly are being tested for improved safety measures to reduce the risk of head injury.

Actually, there have been a number of novel inventions during the past decade that have revolutionized some elements and theories surrounding football equipment.

A player with severely bruised, or even cracked ribs may still be able to play football, thanks to the flak jacket, which features a network of shock absorbing, air-filled tubes encased by a lightweight, plastic shell. And experiments, looking well into the future, have been done with spring-operated pads that will prevent rotation of the knee and disperse any severe shock on the knee joint upward to the leg and upper thigh (which can absorb the impact more easily). Work also has been done on a pulley-operated pad system that works like an automobile seat belt in holding the neck steady during a heavy blow.

Presently it can cost a team as much as $100,000 or more to equip its players for an entire season. Even a simple item such as adhesive tape can entail a considerable expense. Every player has his ankles taped before practice or a game (by league rule), and many players also have other areas taped as well. One NFL trainer estimates that he will use more than 300 miles of tape during the course of a 20-game season, at a cost of nearly $30,000.

Tools of the Trade

FILMS. The use of films probably has affected football coaching strategy more than any other single mechanical innovation since the formation of the league in 1920.

Filming football games in the NFL began in the 1930s and, for a while, it was strictly a hit-or-miss operation. It is now a highly specialized, highly sophisticated skill that demands proficient technicians behind the cameras as well as expert analysts in front of the screens in the darkened coaching rooms around the NFL.

Every NFL game—preseason, regular season, and postseason—is filmed under carefully prescribed limits established by the league, edited under equally rigid instructions, and then broken down into separate reels for offense, defense, the kicking game, etc.

The NFL also has specific rules that govern the delivery of a team's game film to its next opponent—usually the next day.

Film has become the single greatest teaching tool in the game. A player doesn't merely have to take a coach's word about a flaw in his, or an opponent's, style of play; he can see it—over and over, and in slow motion.

Films allow coaches to "grade" players, to give them immediate feedback on their performances. Coaches wear out projectors studying the idiosyncrasies of their own players, as well as individuals on opposing teams, especially when they are considering trade possibilities.

At one time only games were filmed. Now every tryout, mini-camp, or practice is likely to be captured on film. (Film usage, however, has become so costly that experiments with re-usable videotape are under way to determine its economic and practical feasibility.)

In a game film, one camera angle must keep all 22 men on the field in range at all times, so that each play can be broken down in its entirety, and dissected completely, with each player's whereabouts accounted for.

But a different angle might be used on the same play by another camera in order to zoom in tighter on some aspect of the play that might reveal some valuable information the wide angle view would miss.

Teams are constantly experimenting with new camera angles to try and reveal as much information about a play or game as possible. End zone angles, for instance, are greatly appreciated by coaches who want to check spacing within formations, pass defense alignments, and line blocking technique.

COMPUTERS. If films are the most revered tools of football coaches, computers are rapidly becoming number two.

The Dallas Cowboys—the acknowledged pioneers of computer use in the NFL—first began tinkering with computers in 1960. For a while, they were the laughingstock of the NFL. Nobody is laughing anymore.

Every NFL team now relies on computers to some degree, and some teams are almost fanatical about their reliability, application, and benefits.

NFL clubs use computers to process volumes of data on college and professional athletes; to calculate down and distance, and formation tendencies for nearly every imaginable situation; to keep medical records; to compute the payroll and other financial accounts; to keep track of season ticket holders; to imprint tickets; and a constantly expanding list of other assignments.

There is no question that computer printouts have affected strategy in the NFL. Coaches use the computer to measure the rate of success of certain offensive plays against certain defenses (and vice versa), and plot their game plans accordingly. Every NFL coach can enter a game armed with percentage probabilities of what his opponent is likely to do in just about any situation that is likely to develop. And he knows that his peer on the opposite sideline is equipped with similar information about his own team.

Some coaches are cautious about becoming too dependent on computers. They feel there is a danger that the "self analysis" data ob-

```
1ST DOWN
UF SERIES   1ST DOWN    2ND 1-3    2ND 4-6    2ND 7-10   2ND 11+    3RD 1-2    3RD 3     3RD 4-6    3RD 7-10   3RD 11+
RUN PASS    RUN PASS    RUN PASS   RUN PASS   RUN PASS   RUN PASS   RUN PASS   RUN PASS  RUN PASS   RUN PASS   RUN PASS
 27  12     32  13      10   3     12   5     15  12      3   3     5   1     1   5     3   7     2  11     1   6

SCR DRAW    SCR DRAW    SCR DRAW   SCR DRAW   SCR DRAW   SCR DRAW   SCR DRAW   SCR DRAW  SCR DRAW   SCR DRAW   SCR DRAW
  4           2   2                            1          4          1

FIELD POSITION         +G TO +5   +6 TO +20  +21 TO +40  +41 TO -40  -39 TO -21  -20 TO -6  -5 TO -G
                       RUN PASS   RUN PASS   RUN PASS    RUN PASS   RUN PASS   RUN PASS   RUN PASS
                        7   2     14  12     23  17      23  15     26  25     14   7     2

                       SCR DRAW   SCR DRAW   SCR DRAW    SCR DRAW   SCR DRAW   SCR DRAW
                                    2           2  3      1   1      2   3      2

RCVR    TOTAL
        ATT CMP    ATT CMP    ATT CMP    ATT CMP    ATT CMP    ATT CMP    ATT CMP    ATT CMP
  H     17   8                  1         3   1     5   2     8   4
  F     15   9                  1         5   4     2         3   2     4   3
  X     22  11      1           6   4     2   1     4         4   4
  Y      6   3                  2   2     1                   3   1
  Z     13   3                  1         2         3                             2   1
  P1
  PO     1   1                                                                    1   1
  SL     7   3                  1         1   1               3   1     2   1
```

```
LEFT STRENGTH                                              RIGHT STRENGTH
HOLE     5    6    4    2    3    5    7    9               HOLE     8    6    4    2    0    1    3    5    7    9
AVG GAIN 7.0  5.3  4.2  3.0  2.0  1.3  2.4  1.3  2.4  3.2   AVG GAIN      3.2  5.6  4.0       2.3  1.0-2.1  3.4  2.0
FREQ     6    12   19   3    2    3    4    12   6          FREQ     2    0    5    1    1    3    1    12   11   1
```

```
        DESCRIPTION  NBR  DESCRIPTION  NBR  DESCRIPTION  NBR  DESCRIPTION  NBR  DESCRIPTION  NBR  DESCRIPTION  NBR
FAVORITE RUN   24     7   27OUT         6   56            6   14DRAW        5   28BIM         5   37           5
        PASS   60X FADE  2  51PX STRAI  2   61X IN        2   61X OUT       2   71H CROSS     2   129X GO      2
```

NFL teams use computers to learn and analyze their opponents' tendencies — as well as their own.

tained can scare a team out of doing what it does best. And there are some NFL personnel men who still prefer to rely on their basic instincts, rather than simply accepting the data that the computer spits out.

But teams have become so evenly balanced in recent years that it now seems particularly advantageous — perhaps even necessary — to use the computer properly, to gain what every team is constantly seeking: an edge.

Conditioning

With computers, film, the draft, and their administrative responsibilities to occupy them, coaches wind up working all year around.

But an NFL player's "season" really doesn't begin until the opening of training camp in July and can extend — if the player is lucky enough to play for a team that reaches the Super Bowl — until the final weekend in January.

That leaves a period of approximately five or six months of "free" time. So what do NFL players do in the offseason?

Many pursue activities and/or employment that will help them with their careers after football. But very few can afford to divorce themselves from the game entirely.

Most players maintain rigorous offseason strength and conditioning programs to help maintain a physical and psychological edge.

NFL clubs encourage their players to live in or near the city in which they play in order to make it easier to establish regular workout routines with their teammates. Some teams even pay their players small stipends to work out on a regular schedule during the offseason.

Wherever a player spends his offseason, it is absolutely essential that he keep in shape. Conditioning has evolved into a necessary year-round activitiy, and because of the tremendous competitiveness in the NFL today, it has become almost impossible for a veteran to report to training camp hoping to "play his way into shape."

In order to establish more constructive and effective conditioning programs for their players, many NFL teams have enlisted strength and conditioning coaches to establish individual workout schedules. Conditioning needs vary from player to player. A 180-pound wide receiver, for example, is not likely to benefit from the same workout regimen as a 275-pound offensive tackle.

Weight training is a staple of virtually every NFL player's offseason conditioning program. Some players prefer to lift free weights; others opt for the benefits of Nautilus or Universal equipment. But it is as imperative for a player to work to improve his strength and durability in the offseason as it is for him to maintain a weight program during the season. Injuries and lack of strength during the latter stages of a season go hand-in-hand. A tired player is much more likely to get hurt.

Ultimately, durability can be as much of an asset as ability. There have been innumerable players who have survived in the NFL with little more than average talent because they managed to stay healthy.

Some conditioning coaches and NFL players advocate the incorporation of martial arts training, such as Tae Kwan Do (a form of karate), into a conditioning program as a method of sharpening quickness and reflexes. Some players also successfully have used some forms of dance, including ballet, as a means to improve balance and flexibility.

A number of NFL teams now permit offseason basketball teams for their players, who can supplement their individual training programs by competing against local amateur teams, often for the benefit of charities.

A different aspect of an NFL player's conditioning program is his diet. NFL teams take great pains to ensure that their athletes receive proper nutrition by offering team training meals throughout the course of training camp and the regular season. Because of the demands placed on a player's body, because each player's metabolism is different, and because some players are constantly trying to gain weight while others are trying to keep extra pounds off, players' diets often are closely monitored by the team's trainer, who may tailor a special program to suit specific needs.

Being in good condition, finally, is the sum total of many different elements. New theories about all aspects of conditioning sprout constantly. And like the rest of the game of football, conditioning becomes a more scientific discipline every year.

Game Preparation

THE PRESEASON. If a veteran has done his "homework" during the offseason, and reports to training camp in July in good physical condition, all he has to worry about is the sight of several young rookies and free agents who have been invited to the camp to try to take his job away from him.

The opening day of training camps varies from club to club. Most teams begin operation in mid-July. With the exception of quarterbacks and players who have recovered from injuries, veterans are not required to report to camp until 15 days prior to the first preseason game. Rookies usually report a week prior to the veterans.

Most teams without their own regular season training complexes use college campuses (which are not in full session in the summer months) as their bases of operations in the preseason. Campuses feature adequate housing and dining facilities, and can accommodate a football team's special athletic needs.

Once the veterans report to camp, and after a day or two of physical examinations and other administrative chores, teams begin their full double session routine—one practice in the morning and one in the afternoon, called "two-a-days." Occassionally, because of oppressive summer heat and/or humidity, a team will schedule some of its practices at night.

During the early stages of training camp there is a considerable amount of intrasquad scrimmaging. There also are rookie scrimmages with other teams, and controlled scrimmages (with no real importance attached to winning or losing) with other nearby clubs designed to test new players under fire.

Philosophies vary from team to team about the correct roster size for a training camp. Some teams sign hordes of free agents, in hopes of improving their odds of finding one or more that will make the team. Other clubs prefer to work with a more economical number of players.

In any event, it is not unusual for a team to open camp with as many as 100 players. But that figure always gets pared down rapidly to reach a more workable preseason roster.

The beginning of August signals the onset of preseason games, which do not count in the NFL standings. The annual Hall of Fame game in Canton, Ohio (site of the Pro Football Hall of Fame), kicks off the preseason slate of games, followed by a four-game schedule for each club.

The preseason provides a perfect opportunity for some natural geographic rivals to face each other, such as the Jets and the Giants, and the Colts and the Redskins.

A team's first two preseason games usually feature heavy player platooning, as well as experimentation with systems and styles. The initial games also provide a proving ground for players on the fringe, including aging veterans. The final two games are more likely to resemble regular season contests with less shuffling of personnel, as coaches attempt to settle on the right player combinations and develop a winning chemistry.

Success in preseason games doesn't necessarily foreshadow success or failure for the impending regular season. Some teams have been undefeated in the preseason only to wind up flopping in the regular season. Other clubs with poor preseason records have gone on to surprise the league.

GETTING READY TO PLAY. Once the regular season begins, every team settles into a fairly consistent routine of week-to-week preparation. Each club patterns a schedule to fit its own unique needs, but the following routine provides a good example of the typical activity that takes place for most teams leading up to a Sunday game.

1. Monday. The day following a Sunday game usually is a fairly relaxed one for the players. There might be an easy workout (possibly some light running) and injury examinations by the trainers. Also, the players review films of the previous day's game.

2. Tuesday. Very often this will be a day off for the players, but it can be the busiest day of the week for the coaches, who begin putting together the game plan for the upcoming game. Injured players are required to report to the trainer, even on their day off.

3. Wednesday, Thursday, and Friday. These are the longest practice days of the week. Players often will watch films of their upcoming opponent in the morning and then practice hard in the afternoon. Some players also will voluntarily study films on their own (or with a coach) at night. Also, on Wednesday of each week during the season, every NFL team is required to file an injury report with the league office, classifying injured players in one of four categories: 1) probable (roughly 75-99 percent chance of playing); 2) questionable (50-50); 3) doubtful (25 percent); 4) out. These classifications are updated on Thursday, and released by the league to the wire services.

4. Saturday. If a team is playing out of town, much of the day will be devoted to travel. There is usually a light workout without pads. Often there is extra time spent on the special teams. Some teams like to practice in the stadium they will be playing in, or at least on the same type of surface they'll be playing on.

A team's normal routine can change if it is playing in a Monday night game, a Thursday night game, or on a Saturday, but the preparation for a short week doesn't differ much from the regular routine in terms of hours devoted to practice and film study. Usually, just the day

off is changed. For a Monday night game, coaches often designate the previous Monday and Tuesday as days off for the players.

In addition to tuning up their bodies for a game, and digesting the game plan from the coaches, NFL players also undergo a certain degree of psychological conditioning during the week before a game.

There are as many different motivational techniques as there are players and coaches. The importance of mental readiness has never been stressed more in the NFL than it is now; getting an athlete "ready to play" emotionally can be as crucial as preparing him physically.

One of the most interesting recent innovations in mental preparation is the use of isolation tanks, or "mood rooms," which are sensory deprivation climates (often where a player will float on his back in a saline solution) that are especially conducive to enhanced relaxation.

The theory behind the use of such climates is that in a state of heightened relaxation, a player can more sharply focus his mind on his assignments, and concentrate wholly (with no distractions) for several hours at a time on his role in an upcoming game.

The NFL Format
Why do NFL players allow themselves to be put through all this culling, weighing, measuring, practicing, physical strain, and mental conditioning?

As professionals, of course, they are in one sense simply earning a living at something they love; football is their trade. But there is a greater prize.

The ultimate goal for every NFL team when it begins preparations for a new season is to win the Super Bowl. Some clubs, which are in the midst of losing cycles, might be content with just winning a spot in the playoffs, but the Vince Lombardi Trophy, symbolic of supremacy in the NFL, is the pinnacle for every player, coach, and front office worker.

The NFL currently consists of 28 teams.

American Football Conference	National Football Conference
Eastern Division	**Eastern Division**
Baltimore Colts	Dallas Cowboys
Buffalo Bills	New York Giants
Miami Dolphins	Philadelphia Eagles
New England Patriots	St. Louis Cardinals
New York Jets	Washington Redskins
Central Division	**Central Division**
Cincinnati Bengals	Chicago Bears
Cleveland Browns	Detroit Lions
Houston Oilers	Green Bay Packers
Pittsburgh Steelers	Minnesota Vikings
Western Division	Tampa Bay Buccaneers
Denver Broncos	**Western Division**
Kansas City Chiefs	Atlanta Falcons
Oakland Raiders	Los Angeles Rams
San Diego Chargers	New Orleans Saints
Seattle Seahawks	San Francisco 49ers

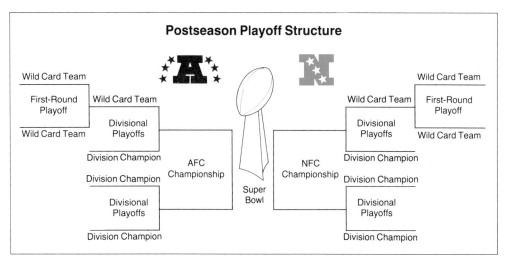

Postseason Playoff Structure

There are two conferences of 14 teams each: the American Football Conference and National Football Conference. Each conference is divided into three divisions: the AFC East, AFC Central, and the AFC West; the NFC East, NFC Central, and NFC West.

Each team plays a 16-game regular season schedule, including two games (home and away) against each opponent within its own division. The teams with the best overall record in each division qualify as division champions and automatically earn a spot in the postseason playoffs.

In addition, the two teams in each conference with the next best records qualify for wild card playoff berths.

In case of ties in the final regular season standings, the NFL has an elaborate tie-breaking procedure to determine division champions and wild card teams.

The playoffs begin with the two wild card teams in each conference facing each other in the first round. The winners advance to the divisional playoffs, which feature games involving the six regular season divisional winners and the two wild card survivors.

The winners of the divisional playoffs then advance to the conference championships. The winner in each conference championship then advances to the Super Bowl.

And for the Super Bowl champion? It gets a chance to try to do it again next season.

Glossary and Index*

audible—A change of plays shouted in code at the line of scrimmage. (14)

backfield—The area behind the line of scrimmage where the running backs set and the quarterback passes. Also the term for the quarterback and running backs.

blindside—To tackle a quarterback from behind as he sets up to pass.

blitz—A pass rush involving defensive backs individually or in combination with linebackers. (**66**)

bomb—A long pass. (39)

bootleg—Deception by the quarterback; he fakes a handoff, then hides the ball against his hip and runs around one of the ends. (**32**)

bump and run—A pass defense technique in which the pass defender bumps the receiver as he comes off the line, then trails him downfield. (**73**)

chuck—A quick shove or push of an opponent who is in front of a defender. The tactic is used primarily against pass receivers. (38, 107)

clipping—An illegal block caused by throwing the body across the back of an opponent. Not called within three yards of the line of scrimmage (close line play). Clipping usually occurs downfield on punts, kickoffs, and interceptions. (**107**, 113)

coverage—Pass defense. Also used to designate the exact type of pass defense used, as in "double coverage." (**19**, 70-73)

*Index page numbers follow definitions in parentheses.
Boldface numbers indicate illustrations as well as text.

crackback—An illegal block thrown by any offensive player who has lined up more than two yards outside the tackle, as he comes back toward the ball. (**110**, 113)

crossbar—The horizontal bar of a goal post over which a field goal or extra point kick must go. (**18**)

cross block—When two offensive linemen exchange assignments, each taking the other's man. Also called a scissors block. (**25**)

cutback—A maneuver by a ball carrier reversing his direction against the flow of a play. (**26**)

dead ball—When the ball can no longer be advanced, it is whistled dead by the officials. Penalties committed after the whistle are called "dead ball fouls."

defense—1. The team *without* the ball. 2. The tactics of that team. (**53-73**, 94-95, 98-99, 102)

defensive backs—The men who play in the defensive secondary; the cornerbacks and safeties. (**10**)

dime—A pass defense that features six defensive backs. (68)

dog—A pass rush involving linebackers individually or in combination. (**66**)

double coverage—Two defensive players covering one receiver. (**68**)

double-teaming—Two offensive blockers working against one defender. (**25**)

down—1. A play from scrimmage; the offense gets four *downs* numbered in sequence, first to fourth, to gain 10 yards and make a first down. 2. When a ball carrier is tackled, his knee touches the ground, or his forward progress is stopped, he is considered *down* and the play ends. 3. On a punt, the kicking team may touch the ball and *down* it at the spot it is touched, ending the play. On a kickoff, the receiving team may *down* the ball in the end zone for a touchback by indicating the kick will not be returned. The

ball is then brought out to the 20. (12, 97)

draft—The annual NFL college player (seniors) selection meeting. (115)

draw—A delayed fake pass play. The quarterback drops back as if to pass, drawing in the defensive linemen. He then hands the ball to a back who runs through the gap left by the defenders. (**30**)

drop—1. The movement of the quarterback after the snap as he retreats into the backfield to set up to pass. 2. The movement of a linebacker as he retreats into pass coverage. (15, **62**) (**19, 70-71, 100**)

encroachment—A penalty called when a player is in the neutral zone at the time of the snap or makes contact with an opponent before the ball is snapped. (107, 113)

end around—A variation of a reverse play in which the tight end or a wide receiver becomes the ball carrier on a sweep. (33)

end line—The line at the back of the end zone. (**9**)

end zone—The area, 10 yards deep, bounded by the goal line, end line, and both sidelines. (**9**)

extra point—The one-point play allowed a team after scoring a touchdown; it may be attempted by run, pass, drop kick, or (almost always) a placekick. Also called the "point after touchdown" (PAT) or "conversion." (18, 80-81)

fair catch—An unhindered catch by the receiver of a punt or kickoff. To signal a fair catch, the player raises one arm high over his head. Once he makes this signal, the player cannot run with the ball nor can he be touched. Penalties are assessed if either occurs. (83, 107, 109, 113)

false start—A penalty called when an interior offensive lineman moves after assuming a three-point stance. A quarterback may also be called for a false start if his signal cadence or actions at the line are judged by the officials to be an obvious attempt to draw an opponent offside. (14, 110, 113)

field goal—A scoring kick worth three points that may be attempted from anywhere on the field. The ball must go between the goal post's uprights and clear the crossbar. (18, **80**-81)

flak jacket—A piece of protective equipment worn to protect against rib injury. (118)

flanker—The wide receiver on the tight end's side of the field; officially a member of the backfield who must set up one yard off the line of scrimmage. (**10**)

flare pass—A short pass to a running back, usually in the flat. (15, 16)

flat—The backfield area near the sidelines. (16)

flea-flicker—A term originally devised to describe a passing gadget play on which a receiver, immediately after catching a pass, laterals the ball to a trailing teammate. It also is now used to identify a number of other gadget plays.

Flex defense—A variation of the 4-3 defense in which two of the down linemen set two to three yards off the line and, instead of charging, stay back and read the play before committing. (**56**)

flood—To put more receivers than defenders in one area of the field. (**39**)

fly pattern—A long pass pattern on which a wide receiver runs full speed downfield. Also called a "go" pattern. (**37, 48**)

force—The defensive responsibility of a safety or conerback to turn a running play toward the middle of the field. (**67**)

formation—The alignment of offensive or defensive players on a play. (**13, 19**)

forward progress—The farthest point of a ball carrier's advancement; a critical factor in the spotting of a ball by the officials after a play, particularly prior to a measurement for a first down.

four-three—A defensive formation featuring four linemen and three linebackers. (**19, 55, 99**)

free agent—A player who can be signed by any club. (116)

free kick—Kick that puts ball in play following a safety (or, infrequently, another kick). It includes kickoffs, safety kicks, and fair catch kicks. (17, 109).

front—A defensive front or front line, such as the four down linemen in a 4-3.

fumble—Loss of possession of the football by the ball carrier, handler, or passer. (112)

gadget play—A trick play. (**33, 50-51, 84-85**)

game plan—The strategy and list of plays chosen before a game. (88)

gap—1. The space between two offensive linemen. 2. A defense with a man in every gap. (**26**) (**56**)

goal line—The vertical plane between the end zone and the field of play that must be touched or crossed to score a touchdown. (**9, 18**)

half—A 30-minute period; two make up a game. (11)

halftime—The 15-minute intermission between the first and second halves of a game. During halftime, teams leave the field, rest, and discuss second-half strategy. (11, 93)

handoff—Giving the ball, hand to hand, to another player. (**15**)

hashmarks—The lines that are used for spotting the ball, located 70 feet 9 inches in from each sideline. (9, 90)

holding—A penalty called for illegal grabbing or grasping of another player. (110, 113)

hole—1. The space opened by blockers for a runner. 2. A numbered space in the offensive line. (**26**)

huddle—A brief gathering for signals by the offense and the defense between plays.

I-formation—The backfield formation featuring two running backs in line directly behind the quarterback. (**13**)

incomplete pass—A pass that is not caught or intercepted. (111)

influence—Deception by the offensive line, denying keys to the defense and leading it away from the play. (30)

inside—The area between the two offensive tackles where running plays can be directed. (**26**)

intentional grounding—A penalty called when the quarterback purposely throws the ball away to avoid being tackled for a loss. (112, 113)

interception—A change of possession when a defensive player catches a pass intended for an offensive player. (16)

interference—A penalty called when either an offensive or defensive player interferes with another player's opportunity to catch a pass. (111,113)

isolation block—A delayed block by a back on a defensive lineman who has been left uncovered. (**25**)

keeper—A play in which the quarterback keeps the ball and runs with it. (**32**)

key—An alignment or movement that can tell a defensive player where the ball is going or what blocks to expect. (**60-62**)

lateral—A toss or pass backward from the direction of play. (16)

lead block—A block by a running back, preceding another running back into the line and hitting the first defender in his path. (**25**)

line call—Signals called at the line of scrimmage, generally by the offensive center, to alert offensive linemen to their blocking assignments. (24)

man-to-man—A type of pass defense where linebackers and defensive backs are assigned a potential receiver to cover individually. (**19, 72, 101**)

midfield stripe—The 50 yard line. (**9**)

misdirection—Deception by the offensive backfield, denying keys to the defense and leading it away from the flow of the play. (**30**)

muff—The touching of a ball by a player in an *unsuccessful* attempt to gain possession of a free ball; no possession is implied. (112)

neutral zone—The space the length of the ball between the offense's and defense's lines.

nickel defense—A defensive formation in which an extra (fifth) pass defender, the nickel back, is brought into the game. (**68-69**, 101)

offense—1. The team *with* the ball. 2. The tactics of that team. (**23-51**, 88-97, 100, 101, 103-105)

offside—A penalty called when a player is across the line of scrimmage at the time the ball is snapped. (107, 113)

onside kick—A short kickoff that carries just beyond the required 10 yards to allow the kicking team a good chance to recover the free ball. (**78-79**)

option pass—1. A play in which the quarterback has the option of throwing to any one of a number of receivers. 2. A play in which the runner has the option to run or pass, and passes. (**39, 47, 48**)

option run—A running play in which the quarterback moves down the line and has the option to hand off, pitch, or run. (**32**)

option runner—A running back adept at rushing without predetermining a hole in the line, allowing him to run wherever he sees open space. Also called "running to daylight." (**26**)

outside—The area outside the two tackles where running plays can be directed. (24)

overshift—A defensive formation in which all or some defensive linemen shift one position over toward the strongside. (**63**)

overtime—The extra 15-minute period added on to regular season games to try to break ties. In postseason games, as many overtime periods as needed are played. Also called "sudden death" or

"sudden victory" overtime, because the first team to score in any manner wins the game. (11, 93)

pass pattern—The route a receiver runs on his way out to catch a pass. (37)

pass rush—The charge to sack or pressure the quarterback as he attempts to pass, by defensive linemen, and sometimes linebackers, cornerbacks, and safeties. (15, **66**) (**102-103**)

penalty—An infraction of the rules that can result in loss of yardage, and/or down, or nullification of a play. (21, 106-113)

penalty marker—The yellow flag thrown by officials to indicate a penalty. (17)

penetration—Movement of defensive linemen across the line of scrimmage.

pinch—A charge by the defensive linemen to the inside. (**64-65**)

pitchout—A long underhanded toss, usually from a quarterback to a running back. (15)

plane of the goal—The imaginary plane extending upward from the goal line that must be broken by a player in possession of the ball in order to score a touchdown. (18)

play action—Plays in which the quarterback first fakes a handoff (a "play fake"), then passes. (**44**)

pocket—The protected area around a quarterback, formed by his blockers, as he passes. (35)

possession—Control of the ball, by an individual or a team.

post pattern—A pass route that goes straight downfield near the sideline, then breaks inside toward the goal post. (**37**)

power sweep—A run around end with both guards pulling to lead the blocking. (**27**)

prevent defense—A defense designed specifically to stop long passes. (105)

pull—When an offensive lineman (usually a guard)

leaves his position to lead a play. (24)

punt—A type of kick used primarily on fourth down that ordinarily results in change of possession. (**17**)

quarter—A 15-minute playing period; four quarters make up a game. (11)

quarterback sneak—A short-yardage play in which the quarterback takes the snap and immediately runs over center.

quick count—An abbreviated signal count used by the offense to initiate a play faster and catch the defense off balance. (14)

quick hitter—A short-yardage, inside running play. (26)

read—1. The quarterback's observation of the defensive alignment at the line of scrimmage. 2. The observation of keys or the action of the offense by a defensive player. (60-62) (**104**)

reverse—A running gadget play in which the quarterback hands off to a ball carrier going by in the opposite direction. There are a number of variations, including passing options. (**33, 51**)

rollout—The action of the quarterback as he moves across the backfield sideways to set up to pass (as opposed to a straight dropback). Also a play based on this action. (44, 48, 49)

rotation—Shifting zone pass coverage to the left or right. (**70-71**)

rule blocking—The coordinated action by offensive linemen to use alternative blocking assignments if the defense changes its alignment. (24)

running lane—The lane parallel to and behind the line of scrimmage used by pulling offensive linemen. (**24**)

sack—When a quarterback is tackled in the backfield by an opposing pass rusher. (16)

safety—A two-point scoring play most often caused by the tackling of a ball carrier in his own end zone, or an offensive penalty in the end zone. (18)

scramble—When the quarterback runs to avoid being sacked. (16, 34)

screen pass—A delayed passing play in which a run is faked and the ball is thrown to a running back or receiver behind the line of scrimmage. (**46-47**)

scrimmage (line of)—The imaginary line running from sideline to sideline through the ball before it is snapped; the line from which a play begins. (8, **16**)

seams—The areas between zones. (**100**)

secondary—The defensive backfield area and/or pass coverage personnel.

set—1. The offensive or defensive alignment. 2. The action of an offensive lineman going into a three-point stance, or the three-point stance itself.

shift—The movement of two or more offensive players before the snap; also can apply to movement by the defense. (**42**) (**63**)

Shotgun—An offensive formation in which the quarterback takes a backward pass from center five-to-seven yards behind the line. (**45**)

signals—The number and word codes called by the quarterback at the line of scrimmage. Signals also are called by the defense prior to a play, usually by the middle linebacker. (14) (56)

situational substitution—Substituting players with specialized skills in specific situations. (94-95)

slant—1. A charge by a defensive lineman to the left or right instead of straight ahead. 2. A running play hitting sharply off guard or tackle. (**64-65**) (**27**)

slant-in—A quick, short pass pattern run diagonally across the middle of the field. (**37**)

snap—The action of passing the ball from the center to the quarterback, punter, or holder to begin a play. Also called a hike.

snap count—The signal on which the ball will be snapped. (14)

sound (going on)—A quick variation of the snap count; the center snaps the ball on the first sound the quarterback utters. (14)

special teams—The offensive and defensive units used on kickoffs, punts, extra points, and field goals. (**75-85**)

spike—When a player slams the ball to the ground after scoring.

split—The distance a player is separated from another player. (**13, 42**)

spot—The placement of the ball after a play or penalty by the referee.

spot of enforcement—The spot from which a penalty or foul is marked off; it varies depending with the situation.

spot pass—A pass pattern predicated on timing and coordination; the quarterback throws to a pre-determined spot on the field before the receiver actually gets there. (**101**)

Spread—1. An offensive formation with no running backs in the backfield. 2. The Dallas Cowboys' term for the Shotgun formation. (**40-41**)

squib kick—A kickoff that is intentionally kicked low and bounces along the field; it can be very difficult to handle. (76)

stack—When a linebacker stands directly behind a defensive lineman. (**64**)

strongside—The side of the offensive formation *with* the tight end. (**10, 28, 58**)

stunt—A planned rush by linebackers and defensive linemen, or by linemen alone, in which they loop around each other instead of charging straight ahead. (**64-65**)

sweep—A run wide around end. (**27**)

three-four—A defensive formation that features three down linemen and four linebackers. (**19, 54, 98**)

time out—A halt to game action called by either

team or the referee. Each team is allowed to call three charged 90-second time outs per half. (11)

touchback—When a ball is whistled dead on or behind a team's own goal line (e.g. on a kickoff that goes into the end zone). The ball is put in play on that team's 20 yard line. (108)

touchdown—A six-point scoring play that occurs when one team crosses the other team's goal line with the ball in its possession. (18)

trap—A running play in which a defensive lineman is influenced across the line of scrimmage, then is blocked by a pulling guard or tackle. (**31**)

two-minute offense—A time-conserving, quick-play (usually passing) attack used primarily in the last two minutes of a game or half. Also called a "two-minute drill" and a "hurry-up offense." (105)

two-minute warning—The notification given to both benches by the officials that two minutes remain in a game or half. (11)

unbalanced line—An offensive formation with a lineman shifted to overload one side of the line. (**28**)

undershift—A defensive formation in which all or some defensive linemen shift one position toward the weakside of the formation. (**63**)

up back—1. A blocking back on a kick play who lines up just behind the linemen. 2. The receiver(s) set in front of the deep receivers on kicks.

uprights—The two vertical poles of a goal post between which a field goal or extra point kick must pass. (18)

waivers—A method of allowing a player either to be claimed by another club or to become a free agent. (116)

weakside—The side of the offensive formation *without* the tight end. (**10, 28, 58**)

zone—An assigned area of pass defense. (**19, 70-71, 100**)

Contributors

Jack Faulkner
Assistant General Manager
Los Angeles Rams
Jack Faulkner has been involved in pro football as a scout, coach, or administrator for more than 25 years. He was an assistant coach with the Los Angeles Rams, San Diego Chargers, Minnesota Vikings, and New Orleans Saints. Faulkner also served on the staff of the Denver Broncos, and was head coach there from 1962-64.

Sid Gillman
Quarterbacks Coach
Philadelphia Eagles
One of the most innovative minds in football today, Sid Gillman's involvement with the game dates back to 1934, when he served as an assistant coach at Ohio State. After an impressive college coaching career, which included head coaching positions at Miami of Ohio and Cincinnati, he took over as head coach of the Los Angeles Rams in 1955. Gillman moved to the AFL in its founding year as head coach of the Los Angeles/San Diego Chargers (1960-69), and ended his head coaching career with the Houston Oilers (1973-74). He worked with the Eagles offense during 1979-1980 and in 1982.

Norm Schachter
Norm Schachter was an NFL official for 29 years, 22 as a referee. He presently works with the league office evaluating, observing, and testing NFL officials. Schachter wrote the *Officials Manual* for the NFL and co-edits *The Official Rules For Professional Football.*

Bill Walsh
Head Coach
San Francisco 49ers
In only his third year as head coach, Bill Walsh transformed the 49ers from a team with the poorest record in the NFL to Super Bowl XVI champions. Walsh worked his way up through the college coaching ranks, including stints at California and Stanford, and entered the NFL with the Oakland Raiders in 1966. He later served with the Bengals and Chargers, then returned to college football in 1977 as head coach at Stanford. He became head coach and general manager at San Francisco in 1979.

The comments of the following NFL head coaches also are gratefully acknowledged:
Mike Ditka, Chicago Bears
Joe Gibbs, Washington Redskins
Bud Grant, Minnesota Vikings
Tom Landry, Dallas Cowboys
Walt Michaels, New York Jets
Chuck Noll, Pittsburgh Steelers
Ray Perkins, New York Giants
Bum Phillips, New Orleans Saints
Don Shula, Miami Dolphins
Bart Starr, Green Bay Packers
Dick Vermeil, Philadelphia Eagles